# The Stone Writer

## Christian Fiction for Young Readers and Teens

### by Toni M. Babcock

Background cover art by Giovanni Cancami
from Shutterstock.com

# Table of Contents

Dedicated to my Grandchildren

# Part One

## Short Stories for Young Readers

# Jacob and the Stone Writer

Across the top of a gigantic sheet of paper, my mom spells out the word: **m-i-s-a-p-p-r-o-p-r-i-a-t-e**. "Okay Jacob, how many words can you make of that?"

She has a tease in her eye when she asks. I think she's putting my ten-year-old brain to the test because she wants me to become a super speller.

I stare at the word. If I switch a couple letters around I can make the word pirate and a lot of little words too, like prop, rope, rap, rim, ate, eat—but it's hard to concentrate.

Today my dog Quincy got out of the yard again. Somebody forgot to latch the gate. I think it might have been me, but I hope not. Our next-door neighbor saw him running along the riverbank. The problem is when Quincy sees people paddling downriver in canoes, or floating by on inner tubes, he'll chase along the riverbank and follow them for miles, but he always comes back—except for today.

I wonder if Mom thinks playing word games will help get my mind off my dog. The fact is, it might be all *my* fault Quincy got lost—and I'm not feeling any better about it.

Late at night I hear a small knock on my bedroom door. It cracks open, and Mom appears in the doorway. "You okay?" she asks.

"Yeah." I don't really mean it, but I say it anyway.

"Anything you want to talk about?"

*What's to talk about? I lost my dog.*

"I don't know, " I tell her. Then I roll over and face the wall.

Mom comes over and sits beside me on the bed. "Don't worry, Jacob."

I sit up and turn toward her. "But Mom, what if something really bad happened to Quincy? What if he's hurt, or what if he got hit by a car?"

"What if he's fine?" She kisses my forehead. "Trust in God. Keep praying, and try to get a good night's sleep."

*Try to get a good night's sleep. Mom always says that.*

"Okay. Goodnight Mom."

"Goodnight Jacob."

She shuts the door and I flop back on my pillow. I lay awake until eleven. Then I get an idea. I'll make a lost dog flyer! We can post them all over town.

I get up, grab my laptop and get started. I have lots of pictures of Quincy stored in my computer, so I pick out my favorite and insert it at the top of a page. Then I type in bold letters: **LOST! - Golden Retriever - Responds to the**

**name Quincy**. I include my address and phone number so people can contact me if they find him.

In the morning I am up early and print my flyers out before breakfast. It's Saturday, and Mom doesn't have to work. We eat and talk about where to post the lost dog flyers. Mom says she can drive me around town. We plan to cover three or four miles and post flyers at Ben Franklin Hardware, Jubilee Grocery, the city park, two gas stations and the Post Office. I hope someone will find Quincy and let me know.

Later around noon, we post the last flyer at the Post Office and I notice an alert tacked on a bulletin board.

"Cougar spotted near the Bren River Corridor at Bennett," the sign reads. "Please leave pets indoors overnight. Attacks on domestic pets have been linked to this sighting."

Mom reads the sign, too—and I think she is reading my mind.

"Come on Jacob, remember what I told you. We have to trust God. Let's take our lunch and eat at the park."

The thought of a cougar attacking Quincy gives me a sick feeling, but I try not to show it. Mom packed us a terrific lunch, and I know she doesn't want me to get too worried about my dog. She's the best.

We eat our lunch and walk the trail around the park. I'm wishing Quincy was here. "Mom, what if that cougar gets Quincy?" I try not to sound too scared. She doesn't say anything at first. Then she picks up a small pine bough from the ground and holds it under my nose. "Smell."

I take a deep whiff. "Ummm, smells good."

Mom crushes the needles between her fingers. "Now smell."

I take another whiff. "Ummm, that smells even better! Like eating candy instead of just smelling it."

Mom laughs, then hesitates and says, "Jacob, God has a reason for everything, even the things that crush us. We can get bitter, or we can allow God to help us grow better. Do you know what I mean?" She takes another whiff of the pine branch.

*Mom doesn't get it. How could God have a reason for me losing Quincy? Or for me forgetting to latch the back gate? I guess she doesn't figure I could ever do something stupid like that.*

"You mean you don't think Quincy might ever come back?" I feel my voice tighten.

"I'm saying we need to accept whatever happens. Besides, sometimes when we think we've lost, we discover something wonderful we never knew we had. Someday God will help you understand."

*Understand what? Mom's just getting poetic again. She's good at that. Whatever she's talking about is not making me feel one bit better.*

Late at night, I keep thinking about what Mom told me in the park. I pray and pray, and ask God to protect Quincy. And I tell God I am sorry for not being sure I locked the gate when I walked out of the backyard. Finally I fall asleep and dream a dream.

In my dream I walk along the seashore, and see a man sitting on the beach. He's dressed like bible-times. He holds a small tool in his hand. All around him are small smooth stones sitting in the sand. He is carving words onto the stones, but I can't tell what the words mean.

"Hello," I say. Normally I would never walk up to a stranger and say hello, but this man is different—like an angel, or like God. I figure he can help me find my dog. "I'm looking for my dog Quincy. A Golden Retriever. Have you seen him?"

The man keeps writing on the stones, but doesn't speak.

10

Why is he ignoring me? "Excuse me," I repeat, "Have you seen my dog?"

The man looks up. "Your dog is in a good place."

"But where is he?"

He puts down his writing tool and stands. He takes a deep breath, looks down, and breathes on the stones. All of a sudden the stones start to vibrate and move! They gather together in a heap, and the man walks over and stands in the middle of the heap. Now I think he must really be Jesus. And if he *is* Jesus, then he knows who left the backyard gate unlatched. Still, he doesn't look mad. He looks kind and wise, and I forget all about Quincy. I'm too amazed. Then a cloud swirls around the man, and he disappears.

My eyes fly open. What did I just dream? I sit up and click on the lamp beside my bed. My favorite rock sits on the nightstand. It's reddish-brown, and shaped like a heart. Mom said she never saw a rock quite like it. I pick it up and hold it in my hand. I wonder what my dream was trying to tell me? Maybe it's telling me God cares about me and my dog. Maybe it's telling me I need to trust him no matter what.

At breakfast, Mom says, "You are awfully quiet today. How did you sleep?"

I go ahead and tell Mom about the stone writer in my dream, and how he breathed on the stones and they came alive. "I think the stone writer in my dream was God. Remember how pastor said God writes his laws on our hearts and makes us want to obey him? Well, God wants me to quit worrying. I figure the stone writer didn't tell me where Quincy was because he wants me to know it's more important to have faith—more important than anything. And even when I make a mistake, God still loves me and wants me to trust him no matter what. Maybe God wants me to write a book about him someday, or be a preacher like Pastor Ramsdale."

Mom sets down her coffee cup and is looking at me like I just dropped in from outer space. Actually, I think she's about to cry.

"You've got a lot to prepare for Jacob," she says. "But when God truly calls, he makes everything fall into place. You'll have to tell Pastor Ramsdale about your dream when you are ready to. He'd love to hear about it."

After church I run ahead of Mom into the house to check messages on the phone. There is just one voicemail, and I punch in the code and listen.

"Mom! They found Quincy along Highway 33!" I holler out the window. "They said they saw my flyer at the Post Office. Quincy is okay!"

"Praise the Lord!" Mom shouts, running toward the back door.

"Wahoo!" I holler. "I can't wait to get my dog back!"

# The Finch and the Fiddle

*Caw! Caw!* Do you know me? I'm Raven—the big black-feathered bird with a large hooked beak. They say I'm loud and can't carry a tune, but I know talent when I see it, and when I first saw old Felix Finnegan playing his fiddle I knew he was no ordinary man.

Felix likes to play his fiddle among the wildflowers where songbirds rest on old-rail fence posts. I often perch on an oak tree limb and listen. On one such day, Felix tapped his toe and played an Irish jig, and a wee yellow finch landed on the fencepost right beside him. The finch was so delighted with the sound of his fiddle she began to twitter merrily along. Soon every day when the old man played, the finch landed nearby and sang her joyful twittering song.

One day a calico cat passed by. It stopped to stare at the delicious little bird, and I knew exactly what the cat had in mind. *"Caw!! Caw!!"* I warned. But the finch was so enthralled with Finnegan's fiddle she didn't seem to hear me.

Felix spotted the cat and stopped tapping his toe. He gave a stern look and pointed his bow. "Don't even think about it," he said.

So the cat twitched its tail and tried to be good, but *meeoowled* as loud and as long as a hungry cat could.

This drew the attention of a shaggy brown dog. When he got to the scene he howled, "Why I'll not be out sung by a finch and a fiddle, and a miserable cat who *meeoowls* in the middle!"

So he sat in the grass and lifted his jowl, and out of his mouth came a ridiculous *howwwl!*

And the cat kept *meeoowling*, and the dog kept *howwwling*.

But the finch and the fiddle didn't stop for caring, they we too busy singing and too busy sharing.

And the little old man and his old wooden fiddle kept right on playing, and didn't fret a diddle.

Just about that time, Cedar Waxwing flew onto a bush of red berries below the tree limb I was perched on. She wore a fine brown tuft on top of her head, and her smooth sleek feathers were perfectly in place. Beside her perched her loyal friend Lark Sparrow. The two songbirds twittered unhappily back and forth about the *meeoowling* cat and the *howwwling* dog, but it was the finch that really seemed to ruffle their feathers.

"Look at Goldfinch," Cedar Waxwing complained. "She's singing with a cat, a dog, and an old man—and whatever that thing is he holds under his chin."

Cedar Waxwing didn't know I was listening from a tree branch just above her.

"I believe that's a fiddle," I interrupted. "And as for the old man, he really is quite talented you know. He's been making music for a very long time."

Cedar Waxwing recognized my noisy caw. "Oh, what do you know about talent, Raven? You can't even carry a tune! Besides, all your cousins are crows and magpies— now that should give you a clue! Whoever the old man is, he should know this is completely unacceptable. Why it's an utter disgrace!"

"I agree," said Lark Sparrow. "A songbird works hard to polish her song. Imagine! Sharing her song with those four-legged beasts and that vain little man and his fiddle."

"Absolutely inexcusable," Ms. Waxwing continued in a huff. "Why we songbirds are graduates of Ms. Cardinal's Outdoor Conservatory of Bird Song. Cardinal would simply pluck out her feathers if she could see such a ridiculous show."

"Indeed, it's very poor," Lark Sparrow added. "And do you know she's a friend to Blue Jay? Everyone knows he comes from a long line of thieves and rogues."

"Don't you two have anything better to do than pick and peck in another bird's business?" I finally cawed.

"If you can't find joy in the song of another, and you won't join in and sing along, why don't you find another place to sing your song?"

"Well!" Ms. Waxwing sniped. "We certainly *will* find another place to sing our song. Someplace where real talent is appreciated!"

And with that, Cedar Waxwing and Lark Sparrow ruffed up their feathers and flew away.

And the cat kept *meeoowling,* and the dog kept *howwwling.*

But the finch and the fiddle didn't stop for caring, they were too busy singing and too busy sharing.

And the little old man and his old wooden fiddle kept right on playing, and didn't fret a diddle.

## The Gospel According to a Pirate

My cousins and I were about to learn the real meaning of Easter in the most unusual way I could imagine. We were all prepared to go on an Easter egg hunt at Grandma and Grandpa's cabin. I was the oldest. Grandma said, "Let's have Jade pass out the Easter bags." After I handed out the bags, I told the kids which trails to take for the hunt.

"Kali, Joe, Nick, and Elena will take Jack Pine trail," I said. "Lucas, Jacob and I will take the bog loop back to the park bench. Olivia, Adeline, and Gemma will take the long trail that starts behind the shed, and Hayden, Peyton, and Cassie will take the trail on the other side of Skinny Swamp. Once you fill your bags, help someone else fill theirs. After everyone is finished, meet back at the campfire. Grandpa has a surprise for us. Ready…Set….Go!"

Each group ran in a different direction, but we could hear each other shouting, "Hey, I found an egg in a woodpecker hole!" or "I found two eggs inside an old stump!"

Kali said she found an egg sitting on the needles of a pine bough, and Peyton found an egg sitting on top of a mushroom.

"Whoa! That mushroom is as big as a pancake!" he said.

There were blue eggs, pink eggs, yellow eggs, and purple. Each egg was filled with raisins, peanuts, candy, or coins. Before long it was time to head back to the campfire.

*"Arrrggg!"* Grandpa said when we returned. "Gather 'round ye lads and lasses."

Grandpa was all dressed like a pirate!

"Grandpa, you look funny!" Kali said.

Grandpa did look funny. He wore a black patch over one eye, and a black pirate's hat on his head. He had a charcoal beard, and when he smiled he had a fake gold tooth that glimmered in the sun.

"Hear me young ones! Gather 'round! I have news to tell ye surely want to hear—*arrrggg!*"

We gathered around, laughing and taunting the "pirate."

"Ahhhh there, ye found yer eggs, have ya?"

Grandpa peered into our bags with his one eye. "Well, *arrrrggg*, think again!" He leaned forward looking mysterious, and pointed toward a trail that led around the pond.

"What's that ye see? Thar's a trail ye missed!"

We all started to run toward it. "Not so fast!" Grandpa shouted. "Hold onto yer skivvies and come back! Ya don't know what yer looking for!!"

"What is it?" I asked, wanting to get back on the trail in a hurry.

"Yer cousin Jade is wanting to know what it is," Grandpa said in a loud voice. Then he bent down, his one eye squinting, looking cautiously from side to side.

"Ya see the 'General' over thar?" He nodded toward a big pine standing at the far end of the pond. "Well, he's guarding a treasure! A golden treasure!  And it's a treasure indeed!  *Arrrggg!*  The General has been keeping watch for some time now, and I'll tell ye this: he don't give up his treasure easy…not fer any old scalawags just looking fer fame and fortune."

"Can we go look for it?" asked Cassie.

Grandpa stood straight and crossed his arms. "So, ye believe there is a *real* treasure over thar do ya?"

Cassie gave Grandpa a skeptical look. "You just said there was!"

"Well, how do ye know I'm not just pulling yer wooden leg? I'm a pirate! *Arrrrggg!*"

"Grandpa! I don't have a wooden leg," Cassie giggled. "Can we go look, please?"

"Well...hmmm......if ye believe it's a real treasure that the General is guarding over thar, then how many eggs will ye give me if I let you find it?"

Cassie thought about it. "I'll give you two eggs!"

"Only two?" Grandpa raised his brow.

Peyton spoke up, "I'll give you *three* eggs!"

"*Arrrrgggg!* Yer brother thar with the flaxen hair is offering me *three* eggs—now who will give me more?" Grandpa turned his squinty eye toward the rest of us.

One by one, we bid away our eggs for the chance to find the hidden treasure.

"I'll give you *all* my eggs if I can find the hidden treasure," Jacob shouted.

"Be it known ye lads and lasses! Jacob is the first to bid away *all* his eggs! I'll take those from ya, laddie." Grandpa reached for Jacob's Easter bag and told him what to do.

"Listen laddie," he said. "Thar be a small shovel beneath the boughs of that tree of which I speak. Find the shovel, and when you do, start ye digging. But I'm warning ya, don't open up the hidden treasure. Bring it to me first, lest ye stir the wrath of the great General! *Arrrrgggg!*"

Everyone ran with Jacob around the pond to the big tree. Lucas spotted the shovel in a clump of grass about ten feet away from the General's roots.

"Over here, Jacob!" he shouted.

Jacob ran over, picked up the shovel and started to dig. He dug deeper, and deeper into the sandy soil. Soon he spotted something gold. "I found it!" he shouted. "I found the treasure!"

Everyone crowded around. Jacob reached in and pulled out a golden-colored egg, a great BIG golden-colored egg. It was sealed shut with tape.

"Remember, don't open it!" I told him.

We all ran back to the campfire. Grandpa was sitting on a log bench looking like a real pirate. He had us gather around like he had something really important to say.

"Now Jacob, hand over yer golden egg fer just a while, and later I will give it back."

Jacob groaned and gave Grandpa a suspicious look, "How do I know you won't steal my treasure? You're a pirate!"

"*Arrrrggg!* I don't need to steal yer golden egg. I have treasure of me own!"

"Okay, five minutes—that's all you get!"

"It's a deal, laddie."

Grandpa held up the golden egg. "Hear ye now ye lads and lasses! Jacob is giving me five minutes to convince ye all that yer all pirates! *Arrrrggg!*"

We laughed and taunted, "We're not pirates! You are!"

"Ohhhh?" Grandpa said furrowing his brow and blinking his sooty eye. "So ya think yer not all pirates do ya? Well… let me ask ya this. Do yer mother and yer father give ye rules to keep?"

"Yes," said Jacob.

"Well then, allow me to ask ye all this. Do yer teachers at school give ye rules to keep?"

"Yes!" We all nodded, rolling our eyes in agreement.

"Well I got news for ya!" said Grandpa gruffly, standing straight. "They don't make rules for people who keep 'em! They make rules for people who break 'em! People like us pirates! *Arrrrggg!*"

Peyton and Jacob fell onto the grass laughing. "You're hilarious Grandpa!"

"Yes sir," Grandpa continued. "So ye best be hearing what I got to say, and quit yer belly rolling in the grass. Arrrrggg! Because I'm here to tell ye that thar's a little pirate in every one of ya. That's why the good Lord gave us rules to keep!  Rules like, ye shall not swear like a pirate, or steal like a pirate, or hate like a pirate, or wish ye had what some other pirate's got—*Arrrrggg!*"

"So sit ye quiet, lads and lasses, and hear what else I got to say. It only takes a little pirate to sink a whole ship. And the bad news is, we're all in the same boat."

We were all listening now to what Grandpa was saying in his silly, crazy pirate way.

"But here's the good news." He held up the golden egg.

"When the good Lord looked down upon us pirates sailing our stormy seas, WE was just what He was looking fer!  We were the treasure he was always wanting for himself, just like this golden egg. 'I'll buy that golden treasure,' the good Lord said!  'I'll buy it with me own blood!'"

"Now the good Lord's name is Jesus, and He gave up all He had and walked the plank fer you and fer me, all the way to the cross of Calvary, and thar He died, but the grave couldn't hold him. No sir…He arose!  And now He lives to claim his prize and live in yer heart and mine. And that's what Easter is all about—*Arrrrggg*!  Now I thank ye all fer listening."

"But Grandpa, what about the golden egg?" Jacob asked.

Grandpa looked at the egg in his hand. "Oh! Ye be wonderin' what's in this golden egg? Well, ye can open the egg after we roast our hot-dogs." Then he handed the egg to Grandma.

"*Wait a minute!* You said I could have it after five minutes!"

"Well no, laddie. I didn't say I was gonna give it back to *you* after five minutes!"

"But you tricked me!" Jacob moaned.

Of course I tricked you! I'm a pirate! *Arrrrggg!*"

*(To be continued...)*

## Jacob Opens the Golden Egg

## (as told by Jacob)

Me and my cousins sat around the campfire roasting marshmallows. The sun had set and the campfire made shadows dance on Grandpa's sooty pirate face.

"Can I have my egg back yet? " I asked. Grandpa knew how much I wanted to open it, but he had another story to tell.

"Hold onto yer skivvies Jacob! ... I knew a pirate once…" he began.

"Another pirate story? " I asked.

"Aye, and it's a good one too, laddie! More interesting than what you think is in that golden egg—*Arrrggg!* "

"As I was saying—I knew a pirate once. His name was Pop-eyed Smitty. One day the good Lord came knocking on old Smitty's heart."

"Let me in," the good Lord said. "I bought ye with my own blood, do ye believe it?"

"No sir! Nobody owns this pirate! I'm the captain of me own ship!" old Smitty said.

Three times, the good Lord knocked, and three times old Smitty hollered back,

"No sir! Nobody owns this pirate! I'm the captain of me own ship!"

"The captain of his own ship indeed," said Grandpa. "Within a year old Smitty and his ship was sunk in a stormy sea—carried off into the cold deep waters where he could hear the Lord knocking no more."

"Now the good Lord has a question for us all. And the question is: Do ye believe ye are the Lord's treasure? And if ye do believe, have ye made the Lord yours? Just like ye looked for that golden egg—have ye searched for Him with all yer heart, calling on Him while He is near, forsaking the pirate way before the stormy seas pull ye far from shore, where ye hear the Lord knocking no more? In other words, if the Lord came knocking, would ye let Him in? Now thar's the question the good Lord would leave rattling in yer bonnie heads until ye get an answer."

We all sat still—staring. Who was this man with the pirate hat? It seemed as if the Lord himself was talking to us in a pirate's voice!

"Well, we've held onto Jacob's golden egg fer long enough. It's about time we let Jacob open it and see what's inside," Grandpa said.

Grandma handed it back to me. "Open it up, Jacob!"

I cracked it open and pulled out a twenty dollar bill buried in a mound of chocolate candy coins! Then a slip of paper fell on the ground.

"See there! Jacob believed the hidden treasure was worth all his eggs, and now he has treasure enough to buy all yer eggs and more!" Grandpa patted me on the back. "Well done, laddie! Ye followed the Lord's example."

He picked up the slip of paper that fell onto the grass. "And here is a promise that goes with the golden egg. It's not just for Jacob, it's for everybody."

*"For God so loved the world, that He gave His only begotten Son, that whosoever believeth in Him, should not perish but have everlasting life, John 3:16."*

"Now thar's a promise ye can believe in! Return to yer play, ye bonnie lads and lasses, but don't forget what the good Lord is saying to you this Easter day!"

# Kali and the Lady Slippers

It's almost Christmas, and me and my best friends Noreen, Melanie, and Katie are together in the Commons after school, waving our take-home papers and talking about the details of our Christmas party.

I read out loud from the paper: "This year, the second through fourth graders will be having a combined Christmas party on December 10th."

"Please bring a Secret Santa gift to share with a girl or a boy. Mark the gift "boy" if you are a boy, or "girl" if you are a girl. The secret is – **No One But You** will know who is giving the gift. Leave your gift at the school office before you go to class, and keep it a **Secret**."

"No way!" Melanie says. "I want to exchange a gift with one of my best friends!"

"Me too," says Noreen.

"Secret Santa gifts are fun," I tell them, trying to look on the bright side. "It's cool not knowing who is going to get the Secret Santa gift."

"But Kali, a Secret Santa should know who is going to get their gift," complained Melanie.

"Well, anyway, it will still be fun!" I tell her. I reach into my pocket. "Hey, I've got enough money to buy each of us a treat at the canteen!"

"Thanks, Kali!" my friends cheer. That gets everyone into a good mood.

Later at home, I ask Mom what I should bring for a Secret Santa gift.

"The party is two weeks from today!" I remind her.

Mom buys toys on sale and gives them away for birthday and Christmas gifts. She has several stashed away in her bedroom closet. She pulls down a board game for me to see.

"How about this? This would make a nice gift."

"What if they already have that game? I better not give that. What else do you have?"

Mom pulls down a jewelry-making kit for girls. "What about this?"

"Cool! I want to give that for a Secret Santa gift!"

"Okay, I'll let you wrap it up. Remember to keep it a secret!"

I choose sparkly paper decorated with snowmen and a pretty red bow. After wrapping my gift, I attach a tag that reads "Girl."

Who will be the lucky one to get my gift?

On the day of the big Christmas party, my teacher Mr. Jensen is in charge. The party is in the school gym. A big Christmas tree stands at one end of the gym. It is covered with colorful decorations we all made in class. The Secret Santa gifts are piled up underneath. A little manger is standing on the other end of the gym, with a doll laying in it like baby Jesus.

Mr. Jensen divides the girls and the boys into two groups by the Christmas tree. We play a game called "Follow the Star." One person in each group is given a big glittery star to hold in front of their team.

Each team is given questions about the Christmas story. If the questions are answered correctly, the whole team gets to step forward five steps. If the questions are answered incorrectly, the whole team has to take two steps back. The first team to "follow the star" and reach the baby Jesus wins the game! Guess what? The girls win!

"Girl power! Girl power!" Me and my friends jump up and down. We love teasing the boys when we win.

"Okay boys and girls, it's time to have the 'Secret Santa' gift exchange," Mr. Jensen announces.

Everyone hurries back to the Christmas tree as fast as they can. Mr. Jensen tells us to form a huge circle and sit down. One by one, he allows each of us to walk up and pick out a gift to open. We have to wait until everyone in the circle has a gift to open before we can open ours.

Noreen picks out a green package with a blue bow. Katie picks a bright pink package with a white bow. Melanie picks out the package I brought, decorated with snowmen all over it and a red bow. I walk up to the tree and pick out a gift wrapped in pretty blue paper with angel designs all over it.

Before we open our gifts, Mr. Jensen says a special prayer of thanksgiving. He thanks God for His gift to us— Jesus our Savior. Afterward, excitement fills the gym as paper is being ripped from gifts around the big circle. Oddly, there is one gift left under the tree. That leaves Mr. Jensen scratching his head. He picks it up and hands it to a sixth grader to take back to the school office.

Katie got a pretty jewelry box. Noreen got a knit cap with a matching scarf and gloves.

Melanie opens her fun jewelry-making kit. "This is so cool!" she says, holding it up for all to see. I smile.

I open my gift and see something inside that looks weird. So I shut the box so no one else can see. Inside the box are old fashioned purple slippers that look way too big.

"What did you get Kali?" Katie asks.

"Uhh…some slippers," I mumble.

"Can we see them?" asks Noreen.

I open the box quickly and say, "See…they are slippers." Then I shut the box.

"They sort of look like lady slippers," says Melanie. "Did you try them on?"

"No." I think my friends can tell I am not very happy about getting purple lady slippers from my Secret Santa.

When I get home from school I plop down on the couch.

"You're awfully quiet, sweetie. How was your party?" Mom asks.

"Okay."

"What did you get from your Secret Santa?"

"Slippers."

I get up and go into the computer room to play a game. I don't want to talk, or even think about those lady slippers. I figure they must have been slippers someone wanted to get rid of. I am so disgusted, I've left them in a bag at the bottom of the steps by the coat closet and don't even bother to show Mom.

When I step out of the computer room, I see her trying on the purple slippers. She has a questioning look on her face. She probably wonders why anyone would give those ugly slippers to anybody for a Secret Santa gift.

At dinner time my family talks about what we can do to help homeless people over the holiday. *I know! Dad manages a catering service!*

"Maybe your company can serve a Christmas meal at the homeless shelter, and I can help!" I suggest. Dad thinks it's a great idea.

"I think we can arrange that," he says.

I have another great idea too. I'll wrap those purple slippers up and give them as a gift at the shelter! I run and get the box of slippers to show Dad.

Dad pulls the fuzzy purple slippers out of the box. He looks at them admiringly. "Those would be perfect," he says. "But isn't this your Secret Santa gift from school?"

"How'd you guess? Anyway, they're way too big," I tell him. "I know someone else will really love these slippers."

Dad smiles. "Well, if you're sure you don't want them, I'll bet some nice lady at the shelter would really like them."

*Want them? I can't wait to get rid of these ugly old slippers. Now I won't have to even look at them,* I secretly think.

At night, Mom finds some new socks to slip into the box with the lady slippers. I wrap the gift in new Christmas paper, and tape a red bow on top. I put a tag on the gift that says: "A Lady's Gift."

On Christmas Eve, I go with Dad to the shelter for the homeless to serve a meal. I serve mashed potatoes. Helping is so much fun! I get to use a special scoop that looks like an ice cream scoop. After I plop a scoop of mashed potatoes on a plate, it goes to another lady who pours hot gravy over the top. Everything smells so good! There is sliced turkey and ham. There is coleslaw, and peas and carrots. There is cranberry sauce and apple pie for dessert.

The people who come for a meal look very poor. There are men with blistered hands. They have scruffy beards and tattered coats.

There are women too, and even children. I wonder how they can live from day to day without bathtubs and washing machines, or even warm beds to sleep in.

There is a tree decorated in the big room next to the kitchen. When it comes time for people to choose a gift from under the tree, I watch from a doorway in the kitchen. I see an old lady in a long grey coat. I notice her worn out winter boots. She carries a dirty duffle bag slung over one shoulder. Her skin is rough and wrinkled. I watch as she sits back and opens a gift—my gift, the purple lady slippers.

I ask Dad if I can go over and meet her. Dad says yes, so I walk right over.

"Hi! Do you like your gift?"

"Oh yes! These are beautiful. And new socks, too. This is just what I need!"

"Why don't you try them on?" I ask.

"Shall I?" She struggles to remove the boots from her feet.

"Let me help!" I kneel down and help pull off her old boots. Her feet are covered with thin, ragged socks. I see little wet sores peeking through the holes.

"Excuse me," she says as she pulls off the old socks and puts on the new ones. She slips the fuzzy purple slippers on top. Now her feet look soft and warm. "Oh, these feel just wonderful. An angel must have put them under the tree just for me!"

I almost tell her I'm the one who put them there, but then I stop myself from saying it. I want to keep it a secret.

At night when Mother tucks me into bed, I tell her what the old woman said.

"She said an angel must have put those slippers under the tree! I didn't tell her it was me." *Wait a minute!* Suddenly I remember there was an extra gift under the tree at school. *Who put it there?*

"Mom, do you think an angel put those purple slippers under the tree at school? When all the presents were passed out, there was still one present left over!"

Mother smiles. "Well, you never know. Angels are always doing God's work, even when we don't know it."

It makes me think how selfish it was for me to be disappointed about getting those old lady slippers, and for wondering how anyone could give such a ridiculous thing for a Secret Santa gift.

"When you say your prayers tonight, be sure and thank God for those slippers!" says Mom.

"Oh, I will!" I tell her, then I give Mother a big hug, and kiss her goodnight.

# The Storm and the Way of the Cross

Kali is the first to hear the blare of the siren's warning, and knows just what to do. "Tornado warning! Everybody in the storm shelter!" she shouts.

She rushes through the house looking for her brothers Jo-Jo and Nicolas, and sister Elena. Mom pulls baby Gemma out of her high chair. Dad is at work. Kali hopes he is safe.

Mom holds a door open to a room with a low ceiling and no windows. It is well lit, and there are a lot of toys to play with, but it is still scary when the tornado siren is blowing. Baby Gemma senses something is wrong and begins to cry. "Don't cry Gemma," says Elena, "We'll be safe."

Everyone files into the storm shelter – except for....Kali. *Where is Kali?*

"Come on Kali!" Mom calls.

"Hold on, I need to find something first!"

"Never mind that, get in the shelter!"

"Just a second, I don't want the tornado to get my picture!"

Soon Mom hears a loud cry coming from Kali's room. "My picture!! No!!! Mom!!! Who did this!!"

Kali runs into the storm shelter with her picture. She flops on the carpet holding it over her chest.

"Why? Why? Why does my stuff always get wrecked?"

"What happened? Let me see it!" Mom takes the picture and turns it over. It is a picture of Jesus hanging on the cross with dark blue crayon scribbled all over it.

Kali is crying. She worked so hard drawing that picture, and she did her very best. It was a Way of the Cross picture she was planning on hanging in the school hallway as part of a special assignment before Easter!

Mom tries to make her feel better. "You're such a good artist, Kali. You can draw a new picture of Jesus that's even better than this!"

"No! I wanted *this* picture to hang at school! Why? Why did this happen?"

Jo-Jo and Nicolas stare at Kali. "I think Elena did it," says Jo-Jo.

"No, we don't know who did it," says Mom. She gives Kali a hug, and quiets her down.

"You know what this reminds me of? It reminds me of how God must have felt after his creation got ruined. In the beginning He made everything perfect, and then sin came in and ruined it, so He knows exactly how you feel," Mom says.

Kali wipes away her tears.

"Your picture is a good reminder of how Jesus took our sin and sorrow on himself, so we could be forgiven and more beautiful than ever. I think your picture is more special now! It makes us stop and think of why Jesus died. And that is what the Way of the Cross pictures are supposed to do, right?"

"Yes," said Kali, "But I guess I better draw a new picture to hang at school. This one is all scribbled."

"Of course, and you can bring this one to school too, and tell your teacher what you learned from it."

"Okay! That's a great idea." says Kali.

As for the big storm, it blew right past the house and disappeared like storms usually do.

# Olivia and the New Girl

Miss Klessing told us a new girl was going to be joining our second grade class the very next day. I wondered what she would be like.

Teacher told us the new girl moved here from Arkansas, so she might talk with an accent. I never talked to a girl with an accent before. I wondered what she would sound like.

The next day the new girl stood next to Miss Klessing in front of the class. She looked a little shy. She had blonde hair, and wore a pretty beaded necklace.

"I'd like to introduce you all to Justine, the newest member of our second grade class. She is excited to visit our lakes in the summer and to make real snowmen in the winter. I hope you will all make her feel welcome!" said teacher.

"Justine, you can sit in that empty desk right across from Olivia," she said.

I smiled at the new girl when she sat down. At lunchtime, I invited her to sit next to me at the lunch table. She didn't talk a whole lot. Maybe she thought the kids would think she sounded weird. I didn't.

"I like your necklace," I told her.

"Thank you," she said. "My ma made it for me."

I noticed she had a matching bracelet on, too. "Did your Mom make your bracelet?" I asked.

"Yep. She makes lots of jewelry. She has boxes and boxes of pretty beads and can make just about anything she puts her mind to. She showed me how to make lots of things. I love making jewelry the most!"

"Cool," I said.

The first two weeks that Justine came to school, I tried hard to make her feel welcome. But somehow Justine kept getting her feelings hurt. Like when a boy named Tommy laughed at her accent and she started to cry.

"Don't let him bother you," I told her. Then I told him to stop it because it wasn't nice to laugh at people's accents.

Then one day, my friend Trisha said the bow Justine wore in her hair looked old-fashioned. Justine heard what she said and pouted for the rest of the afternoon.

"Trisha," I said later, "Please don't say things that hurt Justine's feelings. She cries easy."

Trisha rolled her eyes. "My Mom calls people like Justine 'eggshell' people, because they are so hard to get along with." Then she walked away.

*Oh no,* I thought. *Justine is beginning to make people not like her because she is acting like an eggshell person!*

But there was another problem. Justine started to follow me everywhere I went. If I chose to do something, she would choose the same thing. And if I changed my mind and did something else, she would change her mind too. Pretty soon she wanted to copy everything I did. I asked her not to copy me, but it didn't do any good. She pretended like she didn't hear me. And worse yet, she started to treat me bossy. I started to wish I had fairy wings so I could just fly away from her.

One Friday, I just about had it! I had been putting up with copycat Justine and her bossy ways all week. I didn't want to be mean, but I didn't know what to do. I was standing in line talking to my friend Clare, when Justine cut into the conversation and finished my sentence.

"That is not what I was going to say! I wasn't even talking to you!" I said loudly. Then Justine began to cry.

"Olivia! That was not a kind thing to say to Justine!" Miss Klessing said. "Please apologize to her right now!"

Hot tears filled my eyes. I was sorry for being mean to Justine, but I didn't know what to do about her copying me all the time!

"I'm sorry!" I said to Justine.

The rest of the day I felt awful. Mom asked my why I looked so sad after school, but I didn't want to talk about it. Then I told her.

"Mom, I don't know how to make Justine stop copying me! She follows me everywhere, and copies me all the time!"

"Did you try telling her in a nice way to stop copying you?"

"She won't listen! Plus, she is getting more and more bossy around me. She gets mad if I want to play with someone else. She follows me everywhere. Justine needs to have more than just me for a friend."

"Tonight is school conferences," said Mom. "I think you and I should discuss this with Miss Klessing and come up with a plan."

"But Miss Klessing thinks I am mean to Justine. No, I don't want to talk to her about it!" I felt like crying again.

"Olivia, we need to let her know how frustrated you are about this. Maybe she can help us figure out what to do."

I felt jittery in my stomach the rest of the afternoon. I could hardly eat supper. Later, I looked at the clock. It was six-thirty—almost time to leave for the school conference.

When we got to the conference, Mom brought up the horrible subject of copycat Justine. She explained the whole problem to my teacher while I looked down at my lap.

"Olivia," said Miss Klessing, "You don't need to be afraid to talk about your feelings. Yes, I asked you to apologize today, and I am glad you did. But now I understand some of the reasons why you acted the way you did. Let's think of a way to make Justine just want to be Justine. As long as she thinks she can't be herself and be liked, she will try to be like someone else. That can make other people feel uncomfortable. Is that the way you are feeling?"

"Yes," I told her. "I feel like Justine wants to be me. And it's driving me crazy!"

"Let's see…do you know something Justine might be really good at – maybe something better than anybody else?"

I thought and thought. "Well," I said, "I know her Mom makes really pretty jewelry. Justine says her Mom shows her how to make all kinds of pretty things with her colored beads."

"That's fantastic!" said Miss Klessing. "What if we ask Justine's Mom to come in for a craft demonstration, and let

Justine help our class create a special craft to take home using their beautiful colored beads!"

I smiled! "That would be cool!" *Maybe Justine could learn to be happy just being Justine, and quit following me all over the place.* I felt a little lighter just thinking about it.

"Keep this a surprise," said Miss Klessing. "It will be a surprise for the whole class, a surprise that will help Justine feel good about her special talent at the same time. Promise to keep it a surprise?"

"I promise!" I told her.

On the day of the craft demonstration, Justine was smiling bigger than ever. She was wearing a new beaded bracelet with the letters WWJD printed on big square beads.

"Justine, would you stand up please and show the class your neat bracelet? Boys and girls, this is one of the crafts you will be able to choose from when you decide what you will create. We'll make our craft right after lunchtime," said Miss Klessing.

Justine stood by her desk and held up her wrist with her beaded bracelet. "WWJD stands for, What Would Jesus Do?" she said.

"That is a great reminder," said Miss Klessing. "A bracelet to remind ourselves what Jesus would do in any situation."

At lunchtime it seemed like all the girls were extra nice to Justine. Whatever the reason, it didn't matter. At last Justine had something they wanted, and right now that was all that mattered to me.

Justine's Mom had set out small boxes with different colored beads on a table in front of the classroom while we were at lunch. When we got back to class we got to see them, along with all the colored wires and strings, and stretchy elastic for beading bracelets and necklaces.

During the demonstration, Justine's Mom was really nice. She told silly jokes and stories while she showed us how to bead things. We had so much fun! She let us pick out a favorite charm to keep.

Of course the girls were much more excited over making jewelry than the boys were, but Miss Klessing told the boys to make something special for their Moms or Grandmas, or whoever else they wanted to make something for.

Justine stayed very busy helping her Mom by going from desk to desk, showing us the best way to do our craft. I made a WWJD bracelet just like Justine's.

At the end of the craft time, Miss Klessing announced that once a month, Justine and her Mom were going to meet in the school lunchroom on Saturday mornings to make jewelry and help raise money for earthquake victims. "How many of you would like to help?" she asked. Almost everyone in class raised their hand. Miss Klessing said we could sell the things we made at the end of the year at Grandparent's day, as well as to our family and friends.

I couldn't believe how a bad situation could turn out to be such a good one. Still, I worried if Justine would go back to bossing and following me around again.

The next day I wasn't sure if I should ask her to sit with me at lunch. What if she started following me around and being bossy? Then I looked at my WWJD bracelet. I knew what I had to do.

"Would you like to sit with me at lunch?" I asked her. My stomach did a little flip.

"I can't Olivia! I already promised Kelsey that I would sit with her."

It was working! Justine was making new friends and being happy with just being Justine!

"No problem!" I said. If I was wearing fairy wings that day, I would have flown.

# The Missing Piece

Elena stood in the bathroom doorway at Auntie B's house. "What are you going to do, Auntie?"

"I'm going to clean the toilet. Why do you ask?"

"Well...maybe you don't want to do that."

"Why not?"

"Because...Hayden is playing an April fool trick on my brothers."

Nick and Josiah were Elena's brothers. They came over to play with Auntie's grandson, Hayden. Auntie B. lifted up the toilet seat. Peanut butter was smeared underneath.

"Yukk! This is not very funny," she said. "Too many tricks have been played on me today – and here is a waste of good peanut butter!"

"It wasn't me!" said Elena.

Auntie B. went downstairs to the living room with Elena following. Hayden, Nick and Josiah were sitting on the living room floor, just about to start a puzzle race. Hayden announced he could finish his puzzle faster than they could finish theirs working on one puzzle together.

"No more April fool tricks," Auntie said to the boys. "Hayden, come upstairs and help me clean the peanut butter mess in the bathroom."

"Awww, we were just going to start our puzzle race!"

"But I need your help doing this first," she said. Hayden could tell she meant *right away*.

"Alright," he said. "Don't start until I get back," he told Nick and Josiah. Then he scrambled up the stairs.

"I'll be down in a couple of minutes to make everyone a snack," said Auntie B.

Josiah turned toward Elena. "What did Hayden do?"

"He smeared peanut butter under the toilet seat!"

"No way!" said Nick.

All three ran up the stairs to watch Hayden clean up the peanut butter. They left their cousin Addie alone with the puzzles. (They didn't know Addie could play tricks too.) "April fool!" they said to Hayden as they peered into the bathroom.

"Yeah, yeah," Hayden said as he wiped up the greasy peanut butter. Auntie B. supervised the clean-up operation. Afterwards, they all went back downstairs, and the boys began their puzzle race.

Elena called out the start of the race. "Okay...ready, set, go!"

Hayden worked on one puzzle, and Nick and Josiah worked on the other. Each puzzle had seventy pieces, and it was Elena and Addie's job to cheer the boys on. Hayden's puzzle was Star Wars, and Josiah and Nick's was Batman.

Josiah and Nick were working as fast as they could, but Hayden was still managing to keep just ahead them. "Probably because you've worked on that puzzle a zillion times," Josiah complained.

Just about the time Elena thought Hayden would win the race, she noticed something was bothering him. He started giving an odd look at Nick and Josiah.

"Hey, I'm missing a piece!" he complained.

"Really?" said Nick, hurriedly looking for pieces to finish the Batman puzzle.

"Yeah, *really!*" said Hayden. "You two wouldn't happen to know anything about that, would you?"

Josiah stopped looking for pieces and looked up. "What do you mean?"

"I mean, it's April Fool's Day, and maybe *somebody* hid one of my puzzle pieces when I wasn't looking."

Josiah and Nick looked at each other. "Hey, why didn't we think of that?" they teased. "No, we didn't take any of your pieces," they said.

*"Sure you didn't,"* said Hayden.

Hayden finished his puzzle except for the missing piece, then waited for Nick and Josiah to finish putting together theirs.

Nick popped the last piece of the Batman puzzle into place. "We win!"

"Remember," he said, "Whoever *finishes* first wins!"

"No fair," said Hayden. "I didn't win because you guys hid one of my pieces."

"No way," said Josiah.

"We didn't hide anything – really!!" added Nick.

"I fixed everyone a snack," announced Auntie from the kitchen.

The kids got up and gathered around the dining room table. There were bags of peanuts, and cookies, and homemade fruit smoothies, but Hayden was still bothered about his missing puzzle piece.

"Cheer up Hayden!" said Elena. "I don't think the boys were playing tricks on you. I don't think they hid your puzzle piece."

"Oh, *sure* they didn't," Hayden said, giving the boys a sly look. "My Star Wars puzzle didn't have any missing pieces, right Addie?"

Addie took a sip of her fruit smoothie and shrugged. She didn't want to get in the middle of it. But she had a curious little smile on her face.

Elena walked over to Addie's play kitchen.

"Hey! Look what I found in Addie's frying pan!" Elena held up the missing puzzle piece. She jumped up and down and laughed.

Auntie B. laughed out loud, and the boys began to laugh too.

"Addie! You little stinker!" said Hayden.

"Well, look who gave us the last laugh," said Auntie B. "I think Addie played the best April Fool's trick of all!"

# Lucas

# &

# The Widow of Wicker Woods

"Hey Lucas! Come on up. You can see all the way to old lady Wicker's from up here," Dad said. It was springtime, and I hadn't bothered to climb the big maple tree in our yard since fourth grade started.

I walked over and grabbed hold of the wooden rungs that were nailed to the tree and joined him. Dad pointed out her housetop. Yep. It was old lady Wicker's all right. "Wow, I think we've got the biggest maple tree in town!"

I first heard about old lady Wicker when I was eight. Mr. Bremer, our next-door neighbor told us about her. He's a land surveyor for the county. He said an old woman named Francine Wicker lived alone on the northwest corner of what used to be a good square mile of woods and swamp called Wicker Woods.

"She hung on to that old house," he told us. "She never sold out—said she got it from her folks, and that she planned on dying in it, too. But the rest of the land was sold little by little. In fact, half the land in Woodland Hills belonged to old lady Wicker, even the land your house sits on. It was all Wicker Woods."

Wow. That means my backyard used to belong to old lady Wicker. And this big maple tree with the branches that stretch from east to west used to belong to old lady Wicker. The one with the wooden rungs nailed on, so I can climb up and read my Boxcar books or pretend I'm a squirrel. And the swamp where I like to chase bullfrogs and catch fireflies at night—that used to belong to old lady Wicker too. It's incredible. It's got me thinking—this is one lady I've got to meet.

I like to ride my bike around the neighborhood 'til I get to her house where the grass is too long and the cement steps are crumbling. It's the old grey house that sits up on a hill with a slanted porch that droops down to the side, and with windows that hang between black shutters. It's the house with the paint peeling off and an iron fence around the yard making you feel shut in or shut out, depending on which side you happen to be standing on. Sometimes I see her walking a little dog. I never stopped to say hello. Not yet that is.

Saturday morning, Mom and I leave the house to go shopping. I've already decided what I'm going to get; some new Super Mario games. I ask Mom if we can drive past old lady Wicker's. I figure Mom is curious about her, too.

She says okay, but on the way she asks me not to call her "old lady Wicker."

"Old ladies don't like to be called old ladies," she says. "It's not polite."

"I know, but everybody calls her that–even grown-ups. Why just this morning Dad climbed into the maple tree and said, 'Hey, you can see old lady Wicker's from up here.' That's just what everybody calls her."

"Well, you won't hear me calling her that—the Widow Wicker maybe, or just plain "Francine," but not "old lady Wicker.""

"I'll just call her Mrs. Wicker. What's a widow anyway?"

"Someone whose husband has died, and now she lives alone."

"Well not completely alone," I say. "Some widows have pets, like old lady—I mean Mrs. Wicker. Or maybe they still have grown-up kids at home."

"You're right," says Mom.

Just then, I saw her! "There she is!" I holler from the back seat. "It's Mrs. Wicker walking her dog!"

She is walking along with a little peach-colored poodle.

Mom slows down and stops the car, and I roll down my window and call out, "Hello Mrs. Wicker! I like your dog!"

Actually, I don't know what got into me. I normally don't yell at people out car windows. Mom has a frozen smile on her face. And Mrs. Wicker looks surprised, really surprised—but now she is smiling too. This is terrific!

"Well, thank you young man," she says.

I open my car door and climb out. Mom gets out too. Mrs. Wicker's dog pulls on her leash to get a good whiff of me.

"Her name is Trixie," she says.

I notice Mrs. Wicker is so skinny and short, my dog could pull her flat onto the sidewalk. I never saw her up this close before. She wears a green cotton dress with pearly white buttons. Her hair is wavy—white as snow, and her two front teeth are all crooked and brownish and well, pretty awful.

"Your dog is adorable," Mom says. Then she introduces us and tells Mrs. Wicker we always wondered about the place that used to be called Wicker Woods.

"Lots of people are curious about this old place and the woods that used to be here. Won't you stay a spell? And by the way, just call me Frannie. You might be surprised to hear this, but I've been expecting you."

*There is sure something mysterious about this lady named Frannie Wicker.*

"Can we stay awhile?" I ask Mom.

"Well, okay – if it's not too much trouble."

"No trouble at all," says Frannie. "Come up and sit on the porch. I'll tell you all about Wicker Woods."

Mom and I sit on the porch swing, while Frannie steps into the house. She comes back with a big green book. She sits next to us, plops the book over our laps and tells me I can turn the pages because I am sitting in the middle. The book is full of pictures of Wicker Woods the way it looked a long time ago.

"Wow – there weren't any houses around here except yours," I say, turning the pages.

"That's because our closest neighbors the Turnbalds, lived two miles down the road." Frannie Wicker goes on and on about people and places I never heard of.

The smell of old lady teeth mixed with stale coffee is making me break out in a sweat. I'm seriously ready to slide underneath the big green book and escape with my life, when I see a picture of three kids sitting on the steps of a front porch.

"Hey, that's *this* porch!"

"You're right! And those are my kids: Lucy, Will, and Danny."

Mom's eyes grow wide. "Look Lucas! I can't believe how much Danny looks like you!"

Danny really does look like me. Exactly like me. It's weird. He could be my twin brother  except Danny is around sixty-five years old by now.

"Danny is the reason I was expecting you," said Frannie. Today is his birthday, and I still like to believe he thinks about me on his special day. So when I get a phone call from an old friend I lost track of, or receive an unexpected gift on Danny's day, I like to think its because he is thinking about me. So it was no surprise when a car stopped in front of my house, and a blond blue-eyed boy rolled down the window and called out, "Hello, Mrs. Wicker. I like your dog!"

Hmmm…I figure when people are looking for signs, they are pretty much going to find one, but when I saw

Frannie Wicker walking her dog, I knew I had to stop and say hello—I just had to.

"What happened to Danny?" I ask.

"Danny came down with a sickness they couldn't cure. That's part of the reason for all the houses built around here. We had to sell off the land little by little to help pay for hospital bills. And then my husband got sick, too."

All of a sudden, Frannie changes the subject. "Well now, enough pictures and sad stories. Would you like to see Danny's favorite toy?"

"Sure!"

"Then come with me. I'll show you his room." She sets the green album on a table and leads me and Mom up a narrow set of wooden stairs and into a sunny bedroom. She says she keeps it just the way it was when Danny was there. There is a dresser, and a bed with a small table next to it. Pictures of a boy who looks like me hang on the wall: like me building a sand castle, or getting my hair cut, or sitting on Santa's lap, or riding a bike. It's pretty weird.

Then I see what I think was his favorite toy—a set of soldiers on top of his dresser.

"Is that Danny's favorite toy?" I ask.

"Yes, it is."

Wow. Frannie tells me they're World War II soldiers. They're the coolest soldiers I ever saw. They are metal, and stand about four inches high. Some are kneeling on one knee and have their rifles aimed, and some have their guns slung over their shoulders.

"They belonged to his Uncle Charlie. Each one has a name." Frannie pulls open a dresser drawer and brings out a piece of paper. "Danny wrote the names down, and I saved the list."

She hands it to me. I read the list out loud: "Bulldog, Bailey, Dano, Hatch, Morgan, Corky, Firedog, Ben, Wilson, Max, Dillon and Sergeant Skinner. Wow. Cool names! Hey, there is twelve names, and only eleven soldiers."

"There is," says Frannie, "and that's the mystery. Danny took twelve soldiers into Wicker Woods one day with his friend Alex. The boys came home with only eleven soldiers. Danny told me he buried Firedog behind enemy lines, and they planned on going back in the woods to recapture him the very next day. But the next day, Danny came down with a high fever and had to go to the hospital, and when I asked Alex about the soldier a week or two later, he said he didn't know exactly where Danny buried him. Alex moved away soon after that, and Danny never got well enough to come home."

"So you never got Firedog back?"

"No. Firedog is still buried somewhere, and I don't suppose I will ever get him back."

"I was wondering if you and Mom would like to taste some of my homemade chocolate pudding? I can't eat it all myself! Can you stay a bit?"

Mom agrees we can stay awhile longer.

Frannie takes us to her kitchen where we sit at a small table covered with a blue-checkered cloth. Her creamy chocolate pudding is dee-licious!! But all I can really think about is *where did Danny bury Firedog?*

In the spring and summer I visit Frannie a lot. Sometimes she pays me money for doing jobs like pulling weeds, or picking up trash in the yard. Then I sit in her kitchen and have the best homemade cookies or chocolate pudding in Woodland Hills. And best of all, sometimes Frannie lets me take Danny's soldiers off his dresser and play army with them.

Yep, Frannie is like having another grandma. Sometimes I tell her what's on my mind, and she tries to make me feel better. Like the time I told her about my dog. "Frannie, do you think pets will be in heaven, too?"

"Well, I'm not sure, but there are lots of surprises in heaven. Maybe our pet friends will be one of them, especially since God knows how much they mean to us. I guess we'll just have to wait and see when we get there."

Frannie has a good answer for almost anything I ask her. I decide to ask her something else that's on my mind.

"Frannie, was Alex a good friend to Danny?"

"He was his very best friend. They played together all the time."

"Well...I was just wondering. Maybe Alex really did know where Danny hid Firedog. Maybe Alex dug him up after Danny died, and never brought him back. Maybe he wanted to keep Firedog to remember Danny. I mean, that's what *could* have happened."

"Hmmm....Well, I suppose so, but since I can't believe Alex would lie about it, I'm going to have to believe he was telling me the truth. And if he wasn't telling the truth, *there is nothing hid, that shall not be known,* the Bible says. If Alex took Firedog, then I believe that will be known too."

Like I said, Frannie always seems to have a good answer for everything.

In December, Mom and I show up at Frannie's house to deliver a cake. We knock on the door but there is no answer. We hear Trixie barking like crazy, so Mom opens the door, and we walk in and find Frannie on the kitchen floor!

"Oh, thank God you came! I was praying someone would come!" Frannie says.

Mom decides to call for an ambulance, and they come and take Frannie to the hospital. We take Trixie home with us. We find out later that Frannie broke her hip.

Three days later there is a knock on our door and I answer. It is Frannie's daughter Lucy. She is holding a shoe box in one hand, and a small kennel in the other.

"I'm here to pick up the dog," she says. Mom comes to the door, and Lucy thanks both of us for helping Frannie.

"I don't know what would have happened if you hadn't found her in time."

"How's she doing?" asks Mom.

"Considering her age, very good. The surgery to repair her hip went well."

"We'd like to visit her when she's feeling better," says Mom.

Then Lucy hands me the shoebox. "This is for you. You're very special to my mother – and she wants you to have this."

"Thanks!" I tell her. The box feels sort of heavy.

Mom invites Lucy in, and I sit on the couch with the box.

My sister comes over and sits next to me. "Hey, what did ya get?" she asks.

I pull off a big rubber band and open the box. Danny's soldiers! Bulldog, Bailey, Dano, Hatch, Morgan, Corky, Ben, Wilson, Max, Dillon, and Sergeant Skinner!

"Whoa! I can't believe it. Awesome! Thanks!" I tell Lucy.

"I can't think of a finer boy to take care of Danny's soldiers. We want you to play with them and have fun."

"Cool! I will!" Then I run up to my room to find a special spot to put them. I decide to put them on top of my dresser. Where else?

In May, I get a phone call from Frannie. She is living in a place called Harmony Care Center not too far from my house. She asks if I can check her mailbox at the old place. Frannie still gets her mail there. "I just might be going home soon," she says.

I know what Frannie is thinking. Danny's birthday is May 18th, and she is looking for a letter from an old friend. I hop on my bike and zip over to her house. I step off the bike, lean over and reach into Frannie's mailbox. I pull out a letter. The name on the return address says Alex Turnbald.

Alex? My mind starts to race. I stuff the letter in a bag hanging from my handlebars and speed all the way to Harmony Care Center. I park my bike, take the letter, and run inside past the nurses' station and into Frannie's room. She's sitting in a wheelchair.

"Hello Lucas! Thank you for being my mailman today. What do you have for me?"

"A letter from Alex." I hand her the envelope.

"Alex? Oh my word!"

She removes the letter and begins to read out loud:

*Dear Mrs. Wicker,*

*I bet you never expected to hear from me. I ran into your son Will at a conference in Iowa over the weekend. What a coincidence! He told me you still have your old house. What memories. I'll never forget the fun Danny and I had playing in Wicker Woods. And I remember his birthday is May 18th— which is one reason I send you these greetings.*

*Remember those toy soldiers Danny and I always played with? Danny buried one in Wicker Woods. I think he buried it somewhere near a maple tree. I wish I would have taken the time to try and find him for you. Those World War II soldiers are collectable now.*

*If I am ever up your way, I will stop in for a visit.*

*Take care, Alex Turnbald*

Frannie puts the letter in her lap and sighs. "My, what a sweet man. Imagine! He still remembers that toy soldier. Well, I guess that answers our question about Alex — he really doesn't know exactly where Danny hid Firedog."

There is only one thing on my mind right now: *Firedog is buried near a maple tree, and I am going to find him.*

"Frannie, I have to go home and check something out," I tell her.

"Dear boy, you go ahead, don't spend such a beautiful day here!"

I make a quick exit. I wish my bike could fly! I have a hunch—a big one, and it's getting bigger and **bigger**! Waiting for the light to turn green, my muscles twitch at every intersection.

Two more blocks to go! *Come on Lucas, Go, Go, Go!!*

Finally I get home and park my bike in the garage. I run into the house. Mom is making coffee. "Mom! I need something to dig with, quick!"

"For what?"

"I need to look for something – please, this is really important."

"You're going to be digging in the yard? Where? "

"Back by the old maple tree – I'll leave everything the way it was, I promise – please Mom, I'll explain later!"

Mom finds me a garden tool to dig with. "Here, this should work. I think I better supervise what you are doing. What are you looking for?"

"You'll see." I run outside to the woodsy section in our backyard. I start digging up the dirt near the base of the maple tree – the tree you can climb up and see Frannie Wicker's place from. I dig around the base in a widening circle.

"Lucas, you're tearing everything up! You are going to have to tell me what you are looking for!"

"Firedog, Mom! The missing toy soldier! It's Danny's birthday, and I've got to find him. I just have to!"

Our two dogs run over to see what I'm doing. Mom joins in the search. We pick around that old tree for half an hour. No soldier anywhere.

"Let's go in and clean up," says Mom. "It's time for supper. I'm afraid it's not looking too good for finding a toy soldier around here."

"I thought for sure I'd find him," I moan.

Later Dad tells me, "This yard was totally dug up during construction. Some of the trees were removed. Firedog could be anyplace   right under the surface, or somewhere ten feet under, or in someone else's backyard. There's only a slim chance you will ever find him around here, and Slim just left town."

I go to bed feeling pretty down. I only have one small hope. We live pretty close to Frannie Wicker's place, and if Danny was playing in the woods that day, it could have been the woods in my own backyard.

Summer came and went, and school has a way of making you forget about things. This year I started fifth grade, and I am pretty busy with homework and other stuff. I put my hopes for finding Firedog on hold until spring after the ground thaws out.

In May, Dad decides to build a fire pit in the backyard. We drive to a landscaping store to pick out some big rocks to circle the pit with. I help roll the stones out of the back of Dad's truck and into a wheel barrel. Having a fire pit is going to be cool!

Dad picks a spot to put the fire pit near the back part of our yard. I help him dig a hole about four feet across. Before long, I notice something sticking out of the side of the pit. I dig it free with a stick.

It's a metal soldier! It's Firedog!

"Firedog!" I holler. "Dad! I found him!"

"You're kidding! Let me see." Dad can hardly believe his eyes.

I run to the house to show Mom. "Mom! I found Firedog!"

"What? You found him? I can't believe it. Where was he?"

"I found him in the fire pit where I was digging!"

"No wonder his name is Firedog," Mom says, laughing.

"I've gotta call Frannie!" I can't wait to tell her.

I punch the numbers on the phone as fast as I can...

"Frannie – it's Lucas!"

"Hello Lucas, how are you?"

"Frannie! I found him!   I found Firedog!"

"What? You found him? Why, that's wonderful! Where?"

"I was helping Dad dig a fire pit. That's where I found him – not far from the old maple tree in our backyard."

"Oh my word! And to think you found Firedog today! Isn't that wonderful?"

"Today?" I ask.

"Yes, today…don't you remember? It's May 18th! Danny's birthday!"

"Lucas?... Lucas are you still there?"

(I am still here all right…with my jaw hanging open.)

"Yeah, I'm still here—I just forgot what day it was!"

"Danny's still thinking about me," she says.

 I had to agree, he probably was.

After the phone call, I clean the dirt off of Firedog and place him next to his buddies on top of my dresser. Then I pretend to make the soldiers talk to each other.

"Firedog! You're back!  What happened?" asks Dano.

"I was captured by enemy forces and chained to a post in an underground bunker!"

"How'd ya get out of there?" asks Bulldog.

"I'll tell you how. A lieutenant named Luke rescued me single handed!"

Of course I know better. It was God and Frannie, and the love she has for a boy named Danny. Like Frannie says, *"There is nothing hid that shall not be known."*

# A Horse Called Trouble

Me, Jacob, and Peyton are sort of bored sitting at the cabin taking turns looking into an antique View-Master. One by one, we insert colored slides of The Cisco Kid and Poncho, The Adventures of Tarzan, Hopalong Cassidy, The Lone Ranger, and Gene Autry and His Wonder Horse Champion. Grandpa said they were famous in the old days.

"Lucas, when do you think Grandma and Grandpa will let us have our DS back?" Jacob asks me.

"Remember? They want us to pretend we are in a time warp," I tell him. "We're playing the way kids used to play. We're not getting our DS games back while we are here."

"That's right," added Grandpa. (I guess he overheard me.) "View-Master was as high-tech as we had it back then. And we had to add our own sound effects! Hey, if you guys are bored, you can help me stack firewood. I have a pile of wood outside by the fire pit."

Jacob looks at me. I look at Peyton.

"Uhhh…can we play on the trails first? We want to pretend like we're forest rangers," says Peyton.

"Yeah," says Jacob, "like real forest rangers! Hey, they can call us the Lone Rangers!"

"Yeah! The Lone Rangers! Let's go!" I holler.

"Okay, Lone Rangers, hit the trail – but don't go far, and only stay on our trails," Grandpa says.

"Don't worry, we'll bring a walkie-talkie with us," I tell him, "Just in case we get into trouble." Then we run out the door.

My sister Jade along with my cousins Cassie, Olivia and Kali, are sitting at a table in the clubhouse shed writing a newspaper. They named the paper the *Rock River Review* after the main road through the woods. Today the clubhouse is the Rock River Newsroom.

I grab a walkie-talkie off the workbench, and tell Jade we are the "Lone Rangers," and she should listen for us if we call. Then we three take off down the trail behind the shed.

*Whooosh!!* A bird flies up from the trail in a flash of feathers, and disappears into the woods. *"What was that!?"* I shout.

"A grouse! *Cool!* " says Jacob.

Further on we get to a three-foot-long fence that marks the edge of the property line where the trail turns left. Over the fence the neighbors own a few buildings: two cabins, a tool shed, and an outhouse.

We stop at the fence and look over. No one is around. That's when I spot something strange.

"Hey! Over there! See that? It's a horse! A horse grazing in the tall grass."

It is short and stocky, and has a rust colored coat of hair. As soon as the horse spots us, it brings up its head and perks its ears. Then it trots over toward the fence where we are.

"Don't spook her, just talk quiet." Jacob warns. "This must be the horse Grandma told us about. Grandma says she is friendly, but acts like a puppy dog you can't get rid of."

"Who owns her?" I ask.

"The people who live farther down the road."

"That must be the horse Grandpa tried to ride bare back," says Peyton.

"What was he thinking?" says Jacob.

"I think we should call her Trouble," I tell them.

"Yeah! That's a good name for her," agrees Jacob.

The horse called Trouble walks right up to the fence and lets us stroke her nose. She really doesn't seem like a bad horse, just over-friendly.

"Hey Trouble, you don't seem so bad," we tell her.

A few kind words are all it takes to get Trouble into real trouble. Staying behind the fence just wouldn't do. She walks *around* the fence. Now we are in a fix. Trouble has no bridle on, and no reins to lead her, so she keeps bumping us with her head and her bulky sides.

"I think she wants something to eat," says Peyton.

Peyton pulls a handful of tall grass out of the ground and offers it to Trouble.

She gobbles it up. We all start pulling up grass to feed her. The trouble is, this gets Trouble wanting more grass, so now she is stubbing our toes with her big heavy hoofs and about to knock us over.

*"OOWW!!* Watch out Trouble! Hey, we better get out of here and let her go home," says Jacob.

Unfortunately, Trouble seems to like it better here than her boring old stall. Now she's prancing around in circles, and zigzagging in between us. If we try to get away, she follows us.

"Now what do we do?" Peyton asks.

"Whatever you do, don't run!" Jacob warns. "She'll plow right over you!"

Things are getting scary. "We need help!" says Peyton.

I remember the walkie-talkie in my pocket. I whip it out and made a quick call for help. "Hey! This is Lucas! Is anybody there?" I yell.

After a few seconds I hear the welcome sound of my sister Jade.

"Hey! What's going on?" she asks. Just then, Trouble makes a loud horsey snort.

"Jade! You're not going to believe this!"

"Where are you guys? What was that noise? Did I hear what I *think* I just heard?"

"Ahhh, you mean like a horse? Then you would be correct."

*"Seriously!?!* What are you guys doing with a horse?"

"Good question! I think it escaped!"

My voice is breaking up over the walkie-talkie.

"Actually, we can't get rid of her! *Help!"*

"Where exactly are you guys?"

"We're by the short fence where the trail turns left."

"I've got to see this! We're coming," said Jade.

Soon we see the girls running toward us on the trail. As soon as Trouble sees them coming, she breaks into a trot and starts off toward them.

"Look out!" yells Jacob. "Whoa, Trouble!" he commands. But Trouble keeps going.

"Get off the trail! Hide behind a tree!" he shouts to the girls.

They hide behind trees next to the path, and Cassie yells, *"Whoa!! Horsey!! Stop!!"*

Surprisingly Trouble stops, lowers her head, and walks over to Cassie to check her out. Cassie reaches up to stroke Trouble's nose.

We catch up to Trouble and Jacob says, "We named her Trouble, for obvious reasons."

"Well that's a good name for her!" says Jade.

Then Grandma and Grandpa discover us.

As soon as Grandpa sees the horse he groans. *"Oh no!! Not that horse again!"*

Trouble trots right over to Grandma and Grandpa. "We named her Trouble," I tell them.

"She's trouble all right!" says Grandma. "I want all of you kids to quietly get into the shed, and shut the door," she tells us. "C'mon old girl. It's time to go home." Trouble follows Grandma quietly back down the trail to her stall at the neighbor's where she belongs.

In the meantime, the girls invite us Lone Rangers into the Rock River Newsroom to be interviewed for a feature article in the *Rock River Review*.

"We want a play-by-play description of what happened," Jade says. She asks us questions like, "When did you first encounter the horse called Trouble, and why did you name her that?" While we talk, Cassie records our answers and takes pictures.

"How did you feel when Trouble started acting nutty? Were you afraid?" Olivia asks.

"It was definitely scary," says Jacob.

"How has this changed the way you feel about horses – or has it?" asks Kali.

She sounds like a real reporter. We do our best to answer all their questions in full detail. It's not every day the girls get an opportunity to interview the Lone Rangers, especially after reining in a wild horse and living to tell about it.

"So what did you learn from the horse called Trouble? Anything?" asks Cassie.

"Always carry a walkie-talkie in the woods," I tell her.

"And most important—don't go looking for Trouble," says Jacob "because Trouble will probably come looking for you first!" We all laugh at Jacob's answer.

"This is going to make a great article. What shall we name our story?" Olivia asks.

"I know," says Kali. "We'll name it 'The Lone Rangers run into Trouble!'"

"How about this," says Olivia, "'Trouble runs into the Lone Rangers!'"

"Now *that's* funny!" I tell her. Everyone bursts out laughing!

# The Wing Master

Taramish Twinkle settles light as a feather on the sunny-bright sill of Marianna Miller's bedroom window. Her silky black wings, splashed with their fantastic yellow, orange, and blue design shimmer in the sun.

"It's Taramish, my favorite butterfly!" Marianna whispers excitedly. She opens the bedroom window carefully and leans onto the sill to get a closer look. She secretly wishes she too had silky butterfly wings that could flutter among wild flowers and dance with sparkly dragonflies, or sail happily on the wind just like Taramish.

The butterfly gently waves her wings in the warm sun as if to say, "You are a kind sweet girl, Marianna. The Master has a special plan for you, just wait and see!"

And then, as quickly as Taramish appears, a little breeze catches her up, and she flutters away toward Grandma Mallory's garden patch that grows across the street.

Marianna gets dressed and goes downstairs for breakfast. Mom is stirring up pancake batter in the kitchen.

"Mom," she says proudly, "Guess who landed on my windowsill this morning?"

Mother stops stirring her batter and pauses for a little bit. "Hmmmm, let me think. Was it a little butterfly named Taramish?"

"How did you guess?"

"Oh, I just had a hunch," Mother replies, smiling.

Marianna and her mother have been working all summer on a butterfly scrapbook. They often take a camera to the park or countryside to photograph butterflies in their natural habitat. Then they print out the photographs and paste them into a scrapbook.

Each butterfly has a common and a scientific name, but Marianna likes to give her own names to the butterflies. When they took a photograph of a Black Swallowtail with its beautiful velvety black wings with blue, yellow, and orange markings, Marianna wanted to give it an extra special name.

"Taramish Twinkle!" she decided, "Because it sounds fantastical!"

And best of all, they discovered Taramish fluttering around in their own back yard!

Marianna's beautiful butterfly scrapbook helps her forget about things that make her feel worried or sad. In fact, she has more fun taking pictures of butterflies than she has doing almost anything else! And nobody else can bother her when she is busy working on her scrapbook. Especially people like Serena.

Serena lives three houses down the street. She doesn't seem to like Marianna. No matter what Marianna says or does, Serena always makes it seem like it is a dumb thing for Marianna to say or do. Marianna thinks that is a mean way to treat people, so she avoids being around Serena.

One night, when Mother listens to Marianna's prayers, she is surprised to hear Marianna pray, 'Now I lay me down to sleep. I pray the Lord my soul to keep—away from bossy, stuck-up meanies, especially girls like Serena Sweeny.'

Marianna peeks her eyes open a crack to see Mother's surprised look. Then she opens them, and says, "I'm sorry, Mom, but Serena Sweeny really does act bossy and mean. Otherwise she wouldn't say things to make me feel bad, or think she is so much better than me. I just don't like being around her."

"Well, that's something to pray about," says Mother. "I think God could change her heart, and help you have a change of heart, too. Maybe she just doesn't know how bad she makes you feel."

Marianna wants to believe what Mom says, but she has her doubts.

As for her beautiful butterfly scrapbook, she secretly thinks to herself, *I'm never going to show Serena my butterfly scrapbook. She'll just make fun of it.*

So Marianna keeps her scrapbook a secret, and she keeps Taramish a secret too. In fact, she doesn't tell any of the kids on Benson Boulevard about either one of them.

On Saturday, all the parents in the neighborhood prepare for a big block party. The whole street in front of Marianna's house is blocked off, and there is food and fun outside for all! *Serena won't bother me at the block party,* Marianna says to herself, *she always acts perfect when grown-ups are around.* So Marianna looks forward to all the fun she is going to have.

Mom makes a huge taco salad to share. She carries it outside in a big green bowl, and sets it on a folding table. There are lots of tables set up in the street to hold the food all the neighbors are bringing.

Everything looks so scrumptious! There are pretty fruity-pink whipped cream desserts, plenty of fudge brownies, yummy baked beans and hotdogs, lots of potato salad, and apple crisp and blueberry pie, and bags and bags of snack chips, and of course Mom's wonderful taco salad. Mr. Mallory wears a big white apron and a chef's hat, and is in charge of cooking hot dogs and serving up barbecued chicken.

Some of the tables have games on them like Bingo, Uno, Scrabble, and Guess Who? Lots of kids join in to play. Marianna can't remember having so much fun!

Mom has the neighborhood kids create a fun butterfly memory game called "Wing Master." First, she has them paste pictures of butterflies on cards, two of each kind, and then the kids mix them up and turn them over on a big table. Two players compete against each other, each trying to see who can find the most matching butterflies first. Whoever is the winner gets to pick a prize out of a box. Even Serena thinks it's fun. In fact, she doesn't even get mad when Marianna wins before she does!

*Hmmmm,* Marianna wonders, *maybe God **is** answering prayer.*

Later on, Marianna happily loads her paper plate with chips and a hot dog, when all of a sudden she sees Serena running toward Grandma Mallory's vegetable patch with her arms flailing in the air. Then she hears Serena yell the loudest bossiest yell she ever heard.

"Stop it, Dillon! You're wrecking Mrs. Mallory's garden! Get out of there—NOW!!"

Dillon is Serena's six year old brother, a beady-eyed little boy who always finds some kind of trouble to get into.

"I want to catch that butterfly!" he hollers back.

*Butterfly? What if it is Taramish!* Marianna's eyes grow wide, and her mouth drops open. The paper plate she is holding tips sideways, and the hot dog slips off and lands onto her clean white shoes, ketchup and all—but she doesn't care about that. She drops her plate and runs toward Dillon pleading, "Don't touch that butterfly! You'll hurt it!"

By now Serena is yanking her brother out of the garden by the arm, and Grandma Mallory is walking over to investigate her tomato bush and broken carrot tops, shaking her head in dismay.

Marianna watches Taramish (it really is Taramish) fly over the housetop. *Whew!*

"Dear, dear!" says Grandma Mallory. "With so much fun to be had, surely you children can find something better to do than play in my vegetable garden!"

"We're sorry, Mrs. Mallory! Dillon should know better," Serena says, giving her brother a stern look.

"Tell Mrs. Mallory you're sorry," she says.

"I'm sorry," he mumbles, looking down. But he doesn't look sorry to Marianna.

"Come on Dillon, you're going with me," Serena announces, marching him away.

Marianna blurts out, "Thank you!"

Serena pauses. "For what?"

"For saving Taramish!"

Serena looks puzzled and asks, "Who?"

"Uhhh…I'll tell you later," Marianna says. Then she turns and runs back to clean up the hot dog and chips she spilled on the ground. *Why did I say that? I might have to tell Serena about my secret,* she worries.

At the end of the block party, there is a campfire in Marianna's back yard. The air smells spicy-sweet with the scent of burning wood. It is fun to watch the orange sparks shoot straight up from the campfire, then squiggle and disappear into the night sky. The flickering flames make dancing shadows in the night, and people's happy faces are aglow in its warm light. Dads are laughing and telling stories, moms are making s'mores, and kids are skipping around the campfire like happy hooligans. Even Dillon seems to be cheerful and having a good time.

Marianna roasts a marshmallow on a long stick, when Serena walks over with hers.

"Can I roast marshmallows with you?" she asks.

"Sure!" Marianna moves over to make room for Serena.

They don't talk at first. They just kneel in the grass together, staring into the flames and watching their marshmallows darken and bubble on two wobbly sticks.

"So…." Serena finally asks…"who is Taramish?"

"Oh…just the butterfly your brother was trying to catch," Marianna shrugs. "I like to give butterflies my own names."

She waits for Serena to start in with, "Well that's dumb!" But Serena doesn't.

Marianna continues, "My Mom and I have been collecting pictures of butterflies all summer. We put them in a big scrapbook."

"Really? Can I see it?" asks Serena. By now the marshmallows are charred and black and drooping off the sticks.

"Oops!" says Marianna. The girls laugh and push their marshmallows off into the fire.

"Come on. I'll show it to you!" says Marianna.

The girls set the sticks down and leave the campfire. They run into Marianna's house to look at her scrapbook. Marianna shows Serena her bedroom. There are colorful cloth butterflies hanging from the ceiling. Everywhere in the room are colorful items of purple and blue. "Cool!" says Serena when she walks in.

Marianna's cat Sandy snuggles on a heart shaped pillow on the bed.

"I love your cat!" says Serena, reaching over to pet the cat's sandy colored fur.

The cat meows, then jumps down and runs under the bed.

"Don't mind her, she's shy—and not too friendly," says Marianna. Then she pulls her butterfly scrapbook out of a dresser drawer. "Here it is!" she announces.

The girls sit on a fluffy purple rug and look through the scrapbook pages.

"Hey! There's the butterfly my brother Dillon was trying to catch," says Serena, pointing.

"That's the one I named Taramish Twinkle," says Marianna.

Serena laughs. "Taramish Twinkle—I like that."

The girls admire the beautiful picture of the swallow tail butterfly.

"Did you know that butterfly wings have tiny scales on them that act like little energy collectors?" asks Marianna. "They collect energy from the sun."

"I never knew that," says Serena.

Serena and Marianna talk and laugh for half an hour. Besides both liking butterflies, they discover what else they have in common. Both of them hate centipedes and love cats. Marianna takes music lessons, and so does Serena. Marianna's favorite color is purple, and so is Serena's. Marianna has a hamster in a cage, and so does Serena. Serena has a bossy big sister, and so does Marianna, only Marianna's bossy big sister is away at college.

Suddenly, Mother walks into the room. "Hey you two! I was wondering where you both were hiding."

"Serena wanted to see my butterfly scrapbook."

"Yes, it's really pretty," says Serena.

"Well, it looks like you two are old friends," says Mom.

The girls giggle and agree, and before Serena leaves they make plans to go on their very own butterfly hunt the next day along with Marianna's Mom and her camera.

Marianna has so much to thank God for when she finally goes to bed.

After saying her prayers she says to Mother, "I never thought Serena would want to be my friend, but somehow everything has changed!  We really are a lot alike!"

"Just like two matching butterflies," says Mom.

Marianna laughs, "Yes, just like the game, only God is the greatest Wing Master of all!"

"You are so right," agrees Mom, and she kisses Marianna goodnight.

# The Bully of Buck Hill

When I was eight years old, I learned a lesson about bullies. It started on a windy day, ice cold and grey. I was snowboarding at Buck Hill with my cousin Tommy. The day got colder and colder. We couldn't keep our hands warm anymore. Cold air blasted through our gloves, clamping around our fingers, making our bones ache.

And worse than that, this kid kept trying to make us fall—a big kid in a beat up black leather jacket. He cut us off, and we crashed into a heap, then we stood up, and snow and ice worked its way into our jackets and dribbled down our necks. We brushed off the cakes of snow and looked at the boy in the black jacket laughing at us—the jacket with a red dragon printed on the back.

"Hey Peyton! That kid just cut us off again," Tommy said to me.

"Yeah, I know! He's trying to make us crash into that fence!" I told him.

"Why doesn't he pick on somebody his own size?" he asked.

"Beats me. C'mon, let's go. Besides, I'm freezing. I want to go home," I said.

"Yeah, let's go home. Remember? Your Mom said she was going to bake homemade cookies!"

We carried our snowboards and trudged to the top of the hill. "So long, dweebs!" the kid hollered. We ignored him.

"Let's get some hot chocolate," I said.

"Yeah, that sounds good!" said Tommy.

My Dad met us by the lodge near the food court. "You guys calling it a day already?"

"We're cold. Dad, can we get some hot chocolate?" I asked.

"Sure! That sounds good. Hot chocolate, coming up!"

Dad ordered hot chocolates for me and Tommy at the food court.

"Something happen out there?" he asked. "You seem sort of quiet."

"We're cold, and anyway, some kid just kept cutting us off," I told him.

"What kid?"

"A big kid in a black jacket with a dragon on the back."

I didn't care anyway. We were planning to have a sleepover at my place. We were going to have a blast! On the drive home we talked about our plans for the night.

Later, we sat in the living room and played with our Transformers. We forgot all about the Bully of Buck Hill.

My Mom and Dad are caretakers for the apartment building we live in.

"I have an apartment to touch up and get ready for a new move in," Mom told Dad. "It's Apartment 222."

"When are they moving in?" Dad asked.

"Tomorrow," Mom told him. "They have two boys. One of them is eight. The same age as Peyton. It will be fun having a boy his age to play with right down the hall."

"That's cool," said Dad.

Mom went down the hall to clean the apartment while Dad watched the news.

After all the lights were out, I wondered what the new boy would be like.

After breakfast the next morning, we heard loud talking outside the apartment in the hallway.

"Must be the new people moving in," Mom said.

Me and Tommy were still in our pajamas. We peeked out the apartment door. A big guy with a beard and a tall skinny guy were carrying boxes down the hall.

"Derek – run out to the truck and grab the box marked electronic," one of them called into Apartment 222. A big kid came out into the hall—wearing a black leather jacket. A black jacket with a red dragon printed on the back!

"No way! It's the bully of Buck Hill!!" we whispered to each other.

Yep, it was him alright—big, squinty-eyed and mean. We ran back into my apartment.

"Mom, I thought you said a boy my age was moving in!" I asked her.

"I did. His name is Denny—but he has a big brother, remember? I believe his name is Derck."

Tommy covered his mouth with both hands and started laughing. Then he started jumping up and down laughing, saying "I can't believe it!" I actually didn't think it was *that* funny.

"Oh great," I moaned.

"Why? What's wrong?" asked Mom.

"Oh nothing," I said.

"Well, what is Tommy laughing about then?"

"Well," said Tommy, "the Bully of Buck Hill just moved in next door. No sense hiding the awful truth."

For some reason I couldn't bring myself to blurt out the awful truth.

"Well, he won't get away with much around here," said Mom. "I'm sure he doesn't want his folks to get evicted. Besides, between Dad and your big brother Tyler, I don't think you have too much to worry about from the Bully of Buck Hill."

Yeah…come to think of it, what was I worried about? Derek couldn't touch me! But I still didn't want to walk alone past Apartment 222. Later, after my cousin Tommy went home, I heard a knock on the apartment door. Mom answered it. I heard a boy's voice saying, "Hi, my name is Denny." I ran to see what he looked like.

"Peyton, this is Denny who just moved in down the hall, he wants to meet you!" said Mom.

"Hi," I said. I found out pretty fast Denny was friendly and funny, too.

"I have Transformers, lot's of 'em! Wanna see?" he asked.

Denny wore smudgy glasses, and he smiled big.

"Sure!" I told him.

"Why don't you bring them over to our place?" Mom asked. "You can have supper with us if you like."

"Sure – let me ask my Mom first. I'll be right back!" Then he ran to his apartment.

Denny wasn't mean like his big brother. In fact, by the time summer came, Denny and me were like best friends! But the hard part of having a best friend is, sometimes you learn things about them that make you feel mad, and sad at the same time—like when Denny told me his brother punched him if he didn't do what he said. It made me feel mad because Denny didn't deserve it, and sad because I didn't know what to do about it.

"It's all my fault," Denny told me.

"Why?" I asked him.

"I wanted my brother to think I was cool like he was. So I chewed some tobacco my uncle left at our house. My brother dared me to try it, and I did. Then he was like, 'Whoa…you are in for it now, you little twerp! Wait 'till I tell Mom and Dad what you did!' Then he started telling me I had to do stuff for him, stuff he was supposed to do, or else he would tell Mom and Dad I chewed tobacco."

"Now my brother treats me like his slave, and there is nothing I can do about it."

"That's crazy! Why don't you tell your Mom and Dad what's going on?"

"Are you nuts? He'd beat me up if I did that."

The more Denny talked, the tighter my stomach got. This was the dumbest, craziest thing I ever heard of. It wasn't fair. It just wasn't fair for Denny to be treated that way!

I wanted to tell someone about Denny's problem, but I was afraid. What would Derek do to his brother if he found out I knew about his little secret? *What would he do to me?*

And that's the first thing I learned about bullies. They can make you afraid to talk. It's not fair, but that's what they do, but I didn't want it to be that way—so I prayed about it. I asked God to give me courage and help me know what to do.

First I told my sister Cassie about the problem.

"That's crazy!" she said. "Go tell Dad!"

"How should I tell him?"

"We'll do it together."

We marched up to my Dad, who was watching football.

"Dad?" I asked.

"Hold on a minute," he said.

We watched the quarterback made a fake pass and run the ball all the way to the end zone. Touchdown! We all cheered. Then I got up my courage. "Dad, can I tell you something?"

"Sure, what's up?" Dad turned down the noise of the game.

"Denny has to do everything Derek tells him to."

"Why?"

"Because Derek is holding chewing tobacco over his head," Cassie said.

"What?" said Dad.

"Denny chewed some tobacco to look cool to his brother, now he has to do whatever Derek says, or else Derck will snitch on him," I said.

Dad chuckled. "You've gotta be kidding."

"Don't laugh Dad, this is serious! Denny has been doing all of Derek's chores for almost a year!"

"Oh…so that's why I see Denny lugging out the trash three times a week before his folks get home from work."

"Yep! And that's why Denny has to clean the bird cage and the cat box, and do whatever else Derek tells him to do or he will tell his parents Denny chewed tobacco. It is so unfair!"

"Hmmmm," Dad said. "So this is the Bully of Buck Hill…I get your point. I think I better have a talk with his folks."

"Wait a minute! You better be careful. I don't want to get Denny in trouble with Derek. He might do something!" I said.

"He's already in trouble with Derek. What else is new?" said Dad.

Well, I couldn't much argue with that. My stomach was getting tight again.

"Look, don't worry about it," said Dad. "I'll handle this."

The next day, Denny and my cousin Tommy and I went outside to play near my second floor apartment, so Mom could keep an eye on us from the deck.

It wasn't long before Derek swung open a metal door and came outside looking for Denny.

"You didn't change the cat box," he hollered.

"But you told Mom you'd do it!" Denny answered, like he knew what was coming.

"So what? You're doing it. Get in here now, or I'm telling!" Derek threatened.

"Telling what?" a voice boomed down from the deck just above us. It was my Dad looking over the rail from our 2nd floor apartment!

"What are you going to tell them, Derek? About the tin of tobacco you got your brother to try? About Denny doing all the chores that you are supposed to be doing? Oh yeah, I'm in on the little secret! I think it's time to have a conversation with your dad."

Me and Tommy were scared. We were like, *yikes!* Now what is Derek going to do? But he didn't explode like we thought he would, or spit fire like a dragon, or grab Denny and drag him off to his private beating session. He just stood there speechless, then turned around and went back into the building.

That's another thing I learned about bullies. When someone bigger stands up to them, they usually don't fight back, they just back off and wait for another chance to be a bully (unless they decide not to be anymore).

Dad talked about the situation with Denny's Dad, and from then on, our place became a safe place for Denny to come to. Now that the big secret was out, Denny didn't have to do Derek's chores anymore, and the best news was, Derek stopped punching him.

"Thanks for helping me talk to Dad, " I told my sister. "What if we never said anything?"

"Yeah I know!" she said. "Poor Denny! What if?"

# Fire Ants!

The cabin screen door flew open, and Deanna charged inside. "Where's Benny? I'm gonna kill him!" The tone in her voice revealed a familiar animosity toward her brother.

"You're not going to kill anybody. What's going on?" Mom asked. She set aside the book she was intending to read.

Deanna's eyes flashed angrily around the room. A photo of her father stared blankly from the bookcase as she barreled through the cabin like a storm trooper. The only difference was her father was the real soldier in the family.

"Benny's not here," Mom said as she followed Deanna back out the door, listening to her rage all the way to the bunkhouse.

"He ruined it Mom! Wait till I get my hands on him!"

Deanna held her fingers out in front of her like the claws of a crazed cat. *"Just wait, little brother,"* she hissed. *"You're gonna get it."*

"Deanna, what in the **world** is going on?" Mom demanded. "Benny is not in the bunk house. He biked over to the Hansen's."

She grabbed Deanna and swung her around, "Stop this right now, and tell me what you're so upset about."

"The ant hill, that's what!" Deanna shouted, her voice becoming shrill. "Benny destroyed it! I was going to take photographs for science class, and now it's ruined! See for yourself! It's totally ruined! Wait till Grandpa finds out what Benny did to his ant hill!"

"Calm down!" Mom said, "Let's go take a look."

They took a wooded path around the edge of a small pond to the place where a perfect ant hill once stood. Someone had poked the hill several times with a thick stick. It had collapsed in the center near the top. Hundreds of fire ants were scurrying frantically in and out of the gaping holes trying to repair the damage.

Mom sighed and shook her head. "I sure hope Benny didn't do this. We'll just have to let the ants build up their little city again. I'll get some lath and chicken wire and make a fence around it. Maybe that will help. We'll have to ask Grandpa about it when he comes later. Anyone could have wandered over here during the week and done this. We don't know."

"Mom! Hardly anybody ever walks back here in these woods," Deanna said. She looked across the pond and saw Benny parking his bike near the front porch of the cabin. "Benny, get over here—*Now!*" she shouted.

"Why?" he hollered, catching the distinct impression Deanna was on the warpath.

"You need to see this—hurry up!" she demanded.

Once Benny got to the "crime scene" Deanna began her interrogation.

"Do you know anything about this?" she asked, holding one hand on her hip and pointing the other at the evidence. Benny looked down at the damaged hill.

"I know what you're thinking, and I didn't do it," he said.

"It doesn't sound to me like you're telling the truth, little brother. Do you know what I think? I don't think you *are* telling the truth!" Deanna accused.

"Who are you, Sherlock Holmes, or Dick Tracy?" Benny asked. "I didn't wreck Grandpa's ant hill!" His eyes filled with angry tears.

"Enough! We'll discuss this later," Mom intervened. "You two stay apart until dinner. No more arguing about who did what—and nobody says anything to Grandpa! He'll be here any minute. I'll be the one to bring up the ant hill." Denny and Deanna followed her back to the cabin. Deanna went upstairs into the loft to sulk, and Benny took a stack of Grandpa's old comic books to the bunkhouse.

Later, Mom went to check on Benny. She knocked lightly on the bunkhouse door. "Mom?" he asked.

"It's me," she answered, walking inside. Benny was lounging on a cot, flipping through old comic books and looking dejected.

"I built a fence around the ant hill. It will be fine," Mom said. "Benny, I just want you to know I don't believe you did it. Try to remember Deanna's going through a lot of changes right now, and she's been acting a little dramatic lately."

"A little?" Benny looked up. "Mom! She's acting like a witch! I think she's still mad at me for wrecking her snow fort when I was a kid. I'm eleven, why can't she let it go?"

"Pray Benny. Just pray, and be patient. Things will get better. Fourteen is a hard age for a girl, especially when Dad is away."

"I wish Dad was here, too, but meanwhile she makes a career out of wrecking my life! She yells about a ruined ant hill, and then goes off and ruins the whole day. Besides, she's always blaming me for stuff."

"We'll get to the bottom of this Benny. Trust me. Your sister is going to owe you an apology."

At five-thirty in the afternoon, Grandpa drove into the driveway just in time for Mom's baked chicken dinner and steamy corn on the cob. Benny and Deanna were reminded not to say one word about the fate of the prized ant hill.

After dinner, it was Grandpa's custom to read a portion of scripture, a poem, or a good story at the table. This time, Grandpa chose a portion of scripture he read earlier in the morning during his quiet time.

"I was reading from the book of Ezekiel," he said, putting his glasses on, and opening his Bible. "Here it is: "...I the Lord build the ruined places, and plant that which was desolate: I the Lord have spoken it, and I will do it..."

Deanna gave Benny a not-so-subtle kick under the table. Just wait until Grandpa finds out about the ruined ant hill. What a coincidence! In Deanna's mind Benny was still the prime suspect, and no doubt riddled with guilt.

"As I thought about this passage," Grandpa continued, "I was reminded of the ant hill across the pond. How magnificent of God to create such tiny creatures that work together to form a strong habitation out of the barren sand. Now Deanna, I know you planned to take photographs of my ant hill this weekend for your science class."

"That was the plan Grandpa," Deanna said, her eyes narrowing at Benny. Then she remembered what Mom said, and held her tongue.

"Well, there is something I need to tell you," said Grandpa. "A neighbor up the road stopped over when I was here on Wednesday. His seven-year old grandson was with him. While I was showing my neighbor the new tractor I brought up, the boy started hollering from the other side of the pond.

Poor boy, it was fire ants—he had been poking the ant hill with a stick. He even sat on it! Fire ants started crawling up his shoes and into his clothes. We had to throw him in the pond to scrub him off. Poor little fella! He was bit up pretty bad. I don't think he'll try that again! I'm sorry your photos won't look like much. The ant hill took quite a beating—but it will come back in time."

Deanna sat in mute silence for a few moments. "Oh, that's alright," she finally managed to mutter. "I don't have to take photos of your ant hill. I can get pictures off the internet or somewhere else."

"Well, the mystery is solved!" Mom said cheerfully. "We didn't tell you about it yet Grandpa, but Deanna already discovered the ant hill was damaged. She was afraid her brother did it—imagine that! Deanna, what would you like to say to your brother, now that the mystery is solved?"

Deanna let out a dramatic sigh and confessed, "Alright...I'm sorry Benny. I thought you did it. I don't know what got into me."

"Awww, that's alright. I'll forgive you if you pass the corn while you're eating crow."

"Your sister is apologizing. A little respect is in order Benny," Mom chided.

"That's O.K. Mom, I deserve it," Deanna said.

"I was just kidding 'sis," said Benny. "By the way, I'm sorry I wrecked your snow fort when I was a kid."

"What? I forgot all about that. You're forgiven," Deanna replied.

Mom smiled, holding up her water glass, "Here's to our family, and here's to fire ants!"

Everyone held up their glass and chimed in with a cheer!

# The Promise Pearl

Great-Grandma Pearl used to call me Ruby-girl. She looked a lot like an old Native American. Dry Texas air had weathered her skin to a permanent tan. Deep creases lined her face and neck. She wore her white hair in a single braid down her back. But her eyes were blue. Blue eyes that never lost their twinkle. I used to call her Me-Ma.

When I was small, Me-ma told me an Apache named Grey Hawk traded her Pa a gray dappled horse for a Remington Rifle and a tin of glass beads. She named the horse Stormy. "I had that horse for over twenty years. She was a beauty, a real princess," Me-Ma told me.

By the time I was twelve, Me-ma had taught me just about everything there was to know about horses, and a whole lot of other stuff too. She also told me how it feels to get old. Once, when I was helping her put her shoes on she said, "Ninety-one is a sharp age." I knew what she meant. Getting old hurts.

Me-ma's toes were bent all crazy, making it hard for her to walk. I remember the time she fell trying to get to the couch from her walker. I found her sitting on the floor grabbing onto the couch for dear life. I tried to lift her up, but being I was only twelve years old and a Texas twig like Dad called me, I couldn't budge her.

"Ruby-girl, I'll be alright, just get some help," she said.

I ran out the back door, yelling for Dad, Jake, Mom—anybody! I felt my heart beating fast like a hummingbird floating in mid-air. I remember Mom and Dad bolting out of the barn in a panic.

"What happened?" Mom hollered.

"It's Me-ma! She fell!" I told them.

We all busted through the back screen door and got to her as fast as we could. We lifted Me-ma off the floor and onto the couch. Mom checked her over real good, and said no bones were broken as far as she could tell.

"I went down real gentle—sort of slid," Me-ma told us. "I don't know what happened. My legs just folded up right under me."

That got me thinking. How much longer was Me-ma going to be with us? Every now and then, I'd get this nervous feeling like we were going to have to put her in one of those "cattle barns for old people" like Dad talked about. I always prayed, *Please God, help Me-ma get through one more week, so she won't have to go to one of those places.*

Toward the end of the school year, I had a hard time concentrating. Then my science teacher got my attention. He was all excited, talking about a new scientific discovery. He told us archaeologists found a skeleton of a weird looking fish with a crocodile head, millions of years old. It's the "missing link," he said.

*Wait 'til I tell Me-Ma that Mr. Bailey thinks we came from a fish,* I thought to myself. When I got home, I asked Me-Ma what she thought.

"Well, I guess he's saying that ugly fish crawled out of the ocean and turned into every beast of the field, and every bird of the air—and people, too!"

I could tell Me-ma was getting mad. Dad said it helped keep her blood circulating.

"Over time anything can happen Mr. Bailey says," I told her.

"I'm having trouble taking it all in," Me-ma told me. "Why, those scientists sure have a lot of faith believing all they do. Imagine all that digging, and scratching, and sorting, and speculating, just to prove what they already believe in, so they can convince the rest of us!"

Dad was right. I could see the blood circulating in her cheeks. I laughed and gave Me-ma a hug. "Don't worry," I told her. "I don't believe I came from an ugly old fish."

Me-ma said God is the missing link. I'm siding with her.

One night at supper, I noticed Me-ma having a lot of trouble cutting her food. Nobody said anything, but Mom had a worried look. Everybody was being too quiet—then my brother Jake broke in.

"I heard about a rumble some kids were planning after school. Those guys are busted."

"What do you mean?" I asked.

"They're busted. The cops found out," Jake said, wiping barbecue sauce off his mouth. "I told Fletcher."

Mr. Fletcher is the principal of our school. Right then, I felt proud of my big brother Jake. He's not afraid to do the right thing, even if the kids at school make fun of him.

"Well thank the Lord somebody had the sense to put a stop to that," Mom said. "All this fighting. It's a sad thing." She shook her head.

The next day my brother had the words, "Watch out, **Freak!**" scrawled on his locker with a black marker. It made me mad, but Jake didn't care.

I was so glad when the end of the school year came. No more trash talk scrawled on lockers. No more fights. No more pressure to fit in. Now I'd have all the time I wanted to spend with our horses Sage and Midnight. And I'd have all summer to spend with Me-ma.

In the middle of July, Jake and I walked up the front porch steps of our farmhouse. We just got back from Aunt Juna's ranch where we stayed for a week to help her get ready for the annual Willow Creek Saddle Club Show. Dad told us to go ahead of him. He said Mom had something to tell us.

Mom was sitting in the living room by herself. Me-Ma's chair was empty. Her walker was gone. Something was wrong.

"Where's Me-Ma?" I asked.

"Last night she went to Jesus, Ruby-girl."

Jake walked over to Mom. She stood, and they hugged.

Suddenly the room looked weird, like black and white instead of color. I got dizzy. My throat felt tight. I walked to the staircase and up the steps into my room, like I didn't hear what she said. I didn't want to hear. I shut and locked the bedroom door behind me, and lay back on my bed, staring up at the ceiling. My chest began to heave. I cried, and couldn't stop. Me-Ma was gone to heaven. Me-ma was gone, and never coming back!

I lay there until the sun began to set - until it began to wash a pretty pink hue across my bedroom walls. Me-ma loved to watch sunsets. I sat up to look out the window. It seemed like she was right there with me.

That's when I noticed something sitting on top of my dresser. A red-velvet box. I got up, walked over, picked it up and opened it. Inside was a necklace with a single pearl sitting in a circle of red rubies. An envelope was on the dresser. "Ruby-girl" was written on the front. It was Me-Ma's writing. I pulled out the card inside and read the words she wrote:

*My darling Ruby,*

*When you read this, I imagine I'll be riding a fine horse in heaven. It's about time I got rid of that old walker! Please wear this necklace to remind you of Jesus. Keep him at the center of your life, and remember—where he is, I can never be far away. I love you Ruby-girl, Me-ma*

My eyes filled with new tears. Carefully, I placed the necklace around my neck and locked the clasp. I looked out the window at Sage and Midnight grazing in the sunset down by the corral, and thought of Me-ma riding horseback in heaven. It made me smile.

"I promise," I whispered. "Jesus will always be the center of my life, and Me-Ma—you will never be far away."

The next spring, the school bus dropped me and Jake off on County Road 23 four o'clock in the afternoon. We took off running once we got off the bus, because we could see Aunt Juna's horse trailer parked in the driveway. Mom and Juna stepped out the back porch door as we tore around the corner of the house.

"It's in the barn," Juna announced with a smile. "I got her at auction. I thought you two might like to help me raise her—" Her words trailed off as we ran toward the barn.

There in a wooden stall stood the most beautiful grey dappled horse I had ever seen. "Stormy. That's what we are going to name her," I told my brother before he could even say a word. "In honor of Me-ma." I stepped in her stall and stroked her gently.

"She's a princess, isn't she Jake? Just like Me-Ma's. A real beauty."

# Red Bird's Secret

*Authors note: Red Bird's Secret was first featured in Aletheia, an arts and literary magazine published and edited by Nicholas Muzekari, who also suggested the title for this story.*

When I was a small child I used to think the tall trees whispered secrets to each other in the dark. Now as we float along the narrow banks of Bear Creek I know it isn't so. I am twelve; almost a woman my mother tells me - born in a small cabin near this creek December 10th, 1916. Mother is Ojibwa Indian. Father is a white man. I am White Feather. Everyone calls me Feather.

Today the trees are still, and the air silent. They move quietly as one upon the bank of Bear Creek as our paddles pull us forward through the dark waters before nightfall. Father sits behind me. His red beard glows in the setting sun. He steers our canoe around hidden rocks while Mother paddles in the front. I sit in between among the harvest of rice we have just gathered from the marshes around Bear Creek. The smell of new rice, and the sound of our paddles make me drowsy. Soon, I begin to hear another sound - hollow, like the cry of a loon. It weaves its melody through the trees like a mournful call.

"Do you hear that?" I ask my Mother.

She hesitates…"Red Bird."

"Red Bird?" I ask.

"She is an old woman who lives alone, not far from this place. Sometimes, you hear her play her wooden flute. It is her song."

Mother turns and looks at me. She makes a little smile that seems to cover sadness.

"You have never spoken of her. When did you know her?" I ask.

"Sometime I will tell you - but not now."

I know better than to press my mother for answers when she is not ready to speak.

"An old woman who lives alone - surely she must need things," I suggest. "Can we bring her some rice?"

Father interrupts, "We will speak of giving when the work is done."

He is right. Collecting rice from the marsh is just the beginning of preparations. It must be dried, stirred over a wood fire, and the husks removed. It must be tossed gently in the wind to blow away the chaff. But no work seems too hard when I think of sharing our rice with an old woman who lives alone in the forest.

Late at night I lay still on my bed in a small loft above the kitchen. The light from below casts a soft glow on a picture of Jesus on the wall. When he walked on the land he was treated badly Father told me. I wonder if they treated his mother badly too. An Indian boy once told me my Mother was "bad medicine". I told him that was a lie.

I begin to listen to my parents talking in the kitchen below.

"We will celebrate our own First Rice Feast," I hear Mother say.

First Rice Feast is held every year among the Ojibwa Indians much like Thanksgiving.

"When the rice is prepared, I will take Feather to meet Red Bird. We will invite the old woman to our feast," she tells Father.

I strain to hear what Father will say. Then I hear him ask, "What do you think she will do?"

"No matter. It is time," Mother says. There is a long pause. "Time for Feather to know the truth."

*Time to know what truth? And why is it a secret?* I listen to hear more, but Mother has changed the subject. I am half-excited, and half-afraid.

I peek out the window beside my bed. The tall trees tremble, and seem to whisper in the wind. Are they telling secrets? I feel like a child again, and wonder if I will ever get to sleep.

The next morning at breakfast, Mother tells me we will visit Red Bird the very next week and bring her gifts! Perhaps then she will reveal what the big secret is all about.

Within a few days, I watch as Mother pours our gift of rice into a burlap sack. She fills a tin with wild blueberries, and wraps up some fresh fry bread. Father presents a beautiful wooden bowl and spoon he carved out of birch wood. I convince Mother we must include the extra quilt I keep at the foot of my bed. "It is much too hot in the loft for so many blankets," I insist.

We pack our treasures into two canvas packs and carry them to the creek to load into our canoe. I take Mother's usual spot in the bow of the canoe while she paddles behind in the stern.

After three miles, she begins to scan the shoreline up ahead. Mother is always the first to spot portages in the woods, no matter how hidden they are along the shore.

"You see over there? That's it," she says, pointing.

I see nothing but a solid bank of trees and brush. Then I detect a small rocky ledge, and a narrow opening into the forest. We aim for the opening, and are soon drawing our boat toward the shore, sculling our paddles back and forth. Mother has been quiet most of the trip. After unloading and securing our boat, we hoist the packs onto our backs and Mother leads the way. My curiosity grows with every turn. A black dog meets us halfway along the trail, and runs ahead of us.

Red Bird's house soon appears. It is a small shack, an abandoned trapper's cabin Mother tells me. Its wood has grayed, and the boards at the base are rotted. I wonder how an old woman can keep warm all winter in such a poor place.

Red Bird sees us coming through a small window. Soon her door opens. She appears, smiling, wearing a faded calico skirt and blue shawl. She begins to rattle off words in pidgin English mixed with Ojibwa that I cannot understand, but Mother seems to know perfectly well.

I have never been taught to speak Ojibwa. Mother doesn't talk it at home. She thinks the white people will find out and send me to boarding school to get the "devil's talk" out of me. Father would never let them take me away, but

Mother is still troubled. I cannot understand why the whites are afraid of Indian children speaking Indian?

Red Bird motions for us to come in while she shoos the dog out, jabbering all the while. We sit with her at a small table. I smell cornbread and mint tea. A barrel stove sits in the corner. Red Bird's flute hangs from a leather strap on the wall near the door. Mother and Red Bird continue talking with words I don't understand until I finally break in and say, "What is the big secret?"

They both stop talking and stare at me. Who will speak first? I wonder.

In the next few minutes, I am told a story that turns everything I ever thought about my tribe and my family inside out. I learn Mother was married to an Indian man named Gray Horse many years ago. They had a son who was stillborn. The next year they had another son. He was also born dead. Red Bird, a medicine woman, helped with each birth. Gray Horse believed the deaths were her fault, and so spread rumors among our tribe that she was "bad medicine." I remembered what the Indian boy said to me about my mother, and wondered too… if that is why the tall trees seemed to whisper secrets to each other in the dark.

Not long after spreading the rumors, Gray Horse was pinned under Devil Tooth Rapids and drowned. People believed Red Bird and my mother brought this bad luck to the tribe, and both women were shunned and feared. My Mother was re-named "Stands-Alone." No Indian man would have her after that, and my half-brothers were never spoken of again.

Finally, I understood why our tribe rejected us. They have been afraid of what they do not understand. Fear often makes people act in ways that hurt others. I suppose it is why some whites are still afraid of Indians, and why some Indians are still afraid of each other. Even my mother was afraid of Red Bird, but now she has overcome her fear, and is ready to invite the old woman back into her life.

As we show our gifts to Red Bird, she gives us thanks and quiet tears begin to trickle down her old weathered cheeks. I carry my quilt to her bed and spread it over her thin worn blanket. Mother invites her to our First Rice Feast, and I get an idea. I ask Red Bird to play her flute at our feast!

Later, as we walk the path through the woods back to our canoe I ask Mother, "Why is it that you have never spoken to me of Red Bird, or Gray Horse, or my two half-brothers?"

Mother pauses. "I was afraid to tell you. Once, I knelt beside your brother's graves and a red bird flew and landed a few feet way. I became afraid. From that time on I thought if I told you all these things, you would come under Red Bird's power. Now I know it isn't so. You think our tribe has turned us away - this is only partly true. I have kept you away so you would not find out about the 'curse of Red Bird', but Red Bird has done no harm. She is an old woman, and she is our neighbor. Fear will no longer hold me captive," Mother says.

I look up and take a deep breath of the forest. I close my eyes and listen to the tall trees rustling in the wind. A song bird calls and I feel light as a feather, but I do not feel like a child anymore.

# Part Two:

# The Stone Writer Collection

# Short Stories for Teens

# The Ghosts of Green Lake

Eddie's grandpa drowned the summer of 1936. It was dry and hot, so dry in parts of the country they called it a dust bowl. School was starting in five weeks, and me and my cousin Eddie were both going into the eighth grade.

Eddie was prankish and a terrible tease. He always called me Missy Prissy, but this day he stood red-eyed and pale in the doorway of our kitchen and just said, "Grandpa drowned in Green Lake." The words tumbled out of his mouth and dropped into the air like lead.

"What?" I asked dumbly.

Mom stood up from the table where she was peeling potatoes. She brought her wet hand to her face. "Oh my word! How did it happen?"

Eddie stared past us and spoke flatly, "He fell out of his fishing boat." A flash of remorse spread over his face. "I should have been with him," he mumbled. I could see Eddie's words cut sharp like a razor whip leaving him sore open. He wavered in the doorway, skinny and trembling, his brown eyes looking lost.

"It's not your fault," I told him, stepping forward. Eddie backed away.

"Dear boy, sit down. What can I get you?" Mom said, trying to ease the pain.

"I don't need anything. I just wanted to stop in and tell you. His eyes looked hollow and desperate. "I have to go now... I'm sorry..."

Eddie's voice got small as he excused himself and walked back out the screen door.

"Eddie, wait!" I said, but he didn't stop.

"Pricilla, give him time. I'll call his mother."

I watched Eddie from the porch until his figure got small and disappeared around the trail beside Pine Creek. When I turned around, Mom was already on the phone.

Five years before this happened, Eddie lost his dad to a strange sickness. Nobody seemed to know exactly what it was. That's why Eddie and his mother moved to his grandpa's farm. Eddie and his Grandpa went fishing on Green Lake every summer. After the accident, Eddie changed. He got sullen and hard to talk to. He got mad easy. It seemed something held him like a clenched fist. I only wished I could help Eddie before whatever held him hostage wrecked his life.

There was an old church pew that sat under the big Red Pine between our farm and the farm where Eddie lived. It's where we waited for the school bus every morning. Our school was Green Lake Middle School, which sat up the bank from Green Lake—the same lake where Eddie's grandpa drowned. That's one reason I figure Eddie started skipping school. He couldn't stand looking at that lake.

At least one or two days a week I sat on the pew by myself and thought about what I should do about Eddie. In the meantime, Eddie started hanging around with Leroy Hanks, the worst kid in class. That's when he started punishing everyone who really cared about him. It was almost like he was mad at everybody.

Late in October, Eddie was called into the principal's office for rolling tobacco into cigarettes on school property. I knew I'd miss the bus home if I waited for him, but I wanted to wait, so I sat in a chair by the office and did a reading assignment. It wasn't long before the door cracked open, and Mrs. Callaway the principal invited me inside.

"Come in Pricilla. I think it would be beneficial to have you here."

Mrs. Callaway had bright blue eyes that grabbed and held on until she knew you understood what she meant. Even the bad kids had a hard time being bad around Mrs. Callaway. I closed my book, stepped into her office, and sat in a wooden chair beside Eddie. Mrs. Callaway took a seat behind her desk and began to tell us a story I never heard.

"We had a teacher that taught in a one-room school house right on this hill before the new school was built. Her name was Miss Carlson. Eddie, have you heard of her?"

"Yeah." He hesitated. "She was my Mom's teacher— and Billy's."

"Billy?" I asked.

Eddie rolled his eyes and looked away. "My Mom had a brother Billy who drowned in Green Lake. He was ten."

Goose bumps popped up on my arms.

"How come you never told me?"

"I don't have to tell you everything. Besides, my Mom hardly ever talks about it. That was ages ago."

"It was early winter," Mrs. Callaway continued. "There was a good hard freeze on the lake for several days. Still, your grandmother wasn't sure the ice was safe. Nevertheless, Billy wore her down with his pleading, so she allowed him to have his way and take his skates to school. Unfortunately the ice was too thin that day, and Billy broke through."

Mrs. Callaway paused and looked at Eddie. "How hard was it for your grandmother to forgive herself for letting

Billy take his skates?" Her eyes were piercing and startling blue.

Eddie looked sullen, then just shrugged his shoulders and looked down.

"And what of Miss Carlson?" she continued. "She allowed the younger children out for recess while she stayed behind with the older ones to review an assignment. I'm sure every time Miss Carlson looked down the hill toward Green Lake, she thought of her poor decision. Both of these women had children to raise or children to teach—children who counted on them. They had to forge ahead and not allow regret to interfere with their lives. Am I making sense Eddie?"

"Yeah," he replied, shifting in his chair.

Her gaze softened. "I say we take a walk, the three of us."

She didn't wait for a response, but stood up abruptly.

Eddie and I followed her cue. She led us outside the school building and down toward Green Lake, then over a grassy slope toward the shore.

"What are we doing?" Eddie asked. He didn't want to be that close to the lake. Not yet.

"You'll see," Mrs. Callaway said.

We stopped and sat in the grass overlooking the beach; trees blazed in color reflecting on the water. Mrs. Callaway sat in the grass next to us. She was always so dignified, but at the same time, beautiful and kind.

"Eddie," she asked carefully, "I know you are feeling anguish because you weren't with your grandpa in that boat. But there is something else troubling you. What it is?" she prodded.

Eddie sat with his arms wrapped around his knees. After a long pause, he put his head down, and then made a confession in a low voice, "I hid. Grandpa was calling me, but I figured he could take care of himself. I didn't want to go with him because he had been drinking, so I hid in the barn."

Nobody said anything for a while, then Eddie looked up and stared across the lake.

After a moment or two, Mrs. Callaway said, "I say we throw some stones."

She walked to the waters edge, and picked up a flat, smooth stone. "Regrets haunt," she called out. "They pile up like stones, and weigh us down." She hurled her stone out over the lake and bent down to pick up another. I stood up to join her, while Eddie just sat and watched.

I wonder if she knew Eddie could skip a rock farther than any other boy in Green Lake Middle School. Eddie stood, but kept his hands in his pockets. As I tried skipping stones on the lake, I wondered what Eddie was going to do with the regrets that haunted him. Maybe nothing we said really mattered. Maybe Eddie would always think it was too late for God to forgive him for being afraid to get into that boat. Maybe he thought we were just two silly people whose opinions didn't matter. What if Eddie just turned around and went up that hill, and walked away?

Then a stone whizzed past me and skipped out over the water. It was Eddie's. I took a deep breath and thanked God. Maybe the angry fist was about to let go.

None of us talked much after that, not for a long while. We just kept casting stones out over Green Lake. Eddie seemed to relax. He began to act like his old self again. It all seems so far away now, that warm October day, the day God finally broke through—and pulled my cousin Eddie back from the ghosts of Green Lake.

# The Best Live Nativity Ever

Last November, Miss Jenny gave us an unusual assignment. We each had to figure out a way to raise donations for a local food shelf in time for Christmas. It was our 8th grade "emerging leader" challenge of the year. We would be graded on leadership, originality, and project success.

"Use your imaginations," Miss Jenny said. "I'm excited about what you are going to come up with. Who has a great idea?"

Silence filled the classroom.

Kenny, a boy who sat behind me spoke up. "Have a car wash?"

"In December?" a girl named Marissa asked from the back of the classroom. "I don't think so."

Everybody started laughing.

"The weather is an obstacle Ken, unless you use your originality to work around the problem," Miss Jenny said. "You're the first one to step in and offer an idea. Cars do get dirty in the winter. See what kind of a solution you can come up with. Anybody else?"

Trina raised her hand and offered an idea. "Hand tie fleece blankets and sell them?"

Darla, Trina's friend, made a sour look. "That would be hard to do before Christmas," she said.

"Well," said Miss Jenny, "Nobody says you can't enlist some help. Learning to recognize talent and delegate responsibility is part of what this challenge is all about. Get your whole family involved!"

That got my gears turning. I've got a huge family. Tamara, a girl sitting across from me could tell I was on to something and whispered, "Jade, do you have an idea?"

"Not yet, but when I do it's going to be good."

Miss Jenny sent us home to think of a plan and report back by Friday.

That night I lay on my bed staring at the glow-in-the dark stars I stuck on my bedroom ceiling. There has to be something you can come up with, I said to myself. Something cool and original.

The music of Christmas carols floated up the stairs from the living room.

*"Oh Holy Night...the stars are brightly shining, it is the night of the dear Savior's birth..."*

My mind raced. *Only five weeks till Christmas. Think Jade, think! Please God,* I prayed, *Give me an idea!*

Then, like a star bursting through the sky on a moonless night, I thought of it. Of course! A live nativity! My cousins could play the parts.

I sat up in bed and said out loud, "This is going to be awesome!" Then I stayed awake past midnight making plans for the best live nativity ever.

The next day, I began to make it happen. First, I called my cousin Cassie on the phone.

"I'm organizing a live nativity to collect donations for a food shelf. Would you like to be in it?" I asked.

"Sure!! What do you mean by live nativity?"

"I'm going to have real people dress up to recreate Joseph, Mary and the manger scene and then stage it somewhere. I'm thinking of having it in Kali's front yard, if her Mom will let me," I explained.

"Cool! Who is going to be Mary and Joseph?" Cassie asked. We exchanged ideas.

"Maybe Jacob and Kali?" Cassie suggested.

"That would work. What do you want to be?"

"Ummm…I'll be the angel that announces Jesus birth."

"Yeah, … Let me think this whole thing through and make some more phone calls," I said. "I'll let you know more later on."

After supper that night, I wrote down the names of everyone I thought could play each part. Kali would be Mary. Jacob would be Joseph. Lucas, Peyton and his cousin Tommy could be the three kings. Cassie, Olivia, Elena, Gemma and Adeline would be angels. Nicolas, Jo-Jo, and Hayden could be shepherds. My older cousins could help set up and make sure everything ran smooth for the show. Of course I would have to get everyone to agree with my plan. It was a great plan – so who wouldn't agree?

Everything was fitting together perfectly. Everyone agreed to be just what I asked them to be, except for one person: my brother Lucas.

"Who is going to be baby Jesus?" he asked.

"We are using a doll wrapped in a blanket," I told him.

"But it's a live nativity. If I am playing a real king, there has to be a real baby," he said.

"It will be too cold for a real baby. A doll will be fine," I assured him. "We have to think outside the box."

"Outside the box?" he asked.

"You know… the same as bowling on the Wii. You don't use a real bowling ball. You use a Wii remote."

Lucas looked skeptical. "That's not the same. I don't think I want to be a king."

"Lucas! You'll get to wear a cool costume! Please?" I pleaded. But I knew pleading wasn't going to change his mind, so I went quietly on with my plans hoping he would agree before the night of the big show. By now, Christmas was only four weeks away!

Back at school, Miss Jenny thought my idea was great.

"I have an aunt and uncle who own a goat farm just outside of town," she told me. "I'll see if they would be willing to loan you a couple of goats for your nativity."

"Awesome!" I said. "I have two dogs, and my cousin has a cat. Who says we can't have two dogs and a cat in the stable?"

Miss Jenny laughed. "Nobody! Go for it!"

Grandpa agreed to build a stall and manger for my set. One day I was checking on his progress and I spotted some big sheets of cardboard in the rafters of his garage. "Those would come in handy for extra animals," I told him.

"You're right," he said. "A little paint, a brush, and some talent could turn those into cows, donkeys, or whatever you need. I'll get them down for you."

"Thanks Grandpa. I've only got about four weeks. I better get going!"

I talked to my Sunday-School teacher at church about the live nativity and asked if I could use some robes and other things, like shepherd staffs and crowns from the church's costume department. The church let me borrow almost everything I needed!

Back at home, I was still wishing Lucas would change his mind about being a king, but it wasn't happening—not yet anyway.

One night, when I was sitting on the couch talking on the phone with a friend, Lucas tapped me on the arm and said, "Did you know there may have been more than three kings, and they didn't get to see Jesus until he was about two? So there shouldn't really be any kings in your live nativity. They came later."

I sighed. My brother must have been doing historical research on the Christmas story.

"Lucas, I'm mixing things up a little—you know, making it more exciting for the season. Everyone loves looking at the three kings. It will add more drama."

"Whatever," he said, turning away. Then he looked back and asked, "Hey, do you want to play Monopoly?"

"Later buddy, I'm on the phone right now." I felt a bit guilty for saying that.

In Sunday School, my teacher read us the story of how the carol 'Silent Night' came about. It gave me a great idea.

"Can I have a copy of that story?" I asked my teacher after class. He made a copy for me, and I took it home.

At bedtime I stepped into my brother's room and announced, "Hey Lucas, can I read you a story?"

"Sure. What is it?"

"It's the true story about the song 'Silent Night' and how it came to be.

"Okay," he said, inviting me to sit on the edge of the bed. "I like true stories."

I sat next to him and began to read:

"Long ago in the far away land of Austria, Christmas Eve was fast approaching. But a problem was about to ruin the special music planned for the local church service. The organ had broken and could not be repaired in time.

Was it mice or rust that chewed away on the organ pipes? No one knows for sure, but Joseph Mohr, the man in charge, had to think of a way to make music for the midnight service. That Christmas Eve in 1818, he journeyed to the home of a musician named Franz Gruber, who lived nearby. Joseph carried a poem he had written with him. He hoped Franz could put it to guitar music.

*If we don't have an organ to sing praises to God, we will use my guitar instead,* Joseph Mohr decided.

Franz Gruber created a simple tune for the guitar that would fit the words of the poem perfect—the words we know so well:

*"Silent night—Holy night, all is calm, all is bright, Round yon virgin, Mother and Child*

*Holy Infant so tender and mild, Sleep in heavenly peace—Sleep in heavenly peace."*

"Wasn't that a great story?" I asked Lucas.

"Yeah. I like the part where he thought of using a guitar, just in time for Christmas Eve."

"Because everything couldn't be perfect the way he wanted it to be, so he had to come up with another plan," I reminded him.

"Right…" Lucas' eyes stared into mine, and I think he understood. The live nativity didn't have to be "perfect." We could use a doll instead of a real baby.

And I decided Lucas didn't have to be a king either. Plans change. I'd make Jo-Jo a king instead.

"Lucas, I've been thinking. You don't have to be a king if you don't want to. I'll switch things around, and make it work anyway. What we really need is—something that will attract a crowd. You know… like music. Mom can play the guitar and...are you thinking what I'm thinking?"

"You mean have Mom play 'Silent Night' on the guitar like in the story?" Lucas asked.

"I mean have Mom play 'Silent Night' on the guitar, and you sing it."

I knew my brother Lucas had a good voice. This was a no brainer. "You could dress up in regular clothes. With guitar music and your song, we'll collect more food for the food shelf!" I told him.

Lucas looked off into space, and his face broke into a smile. "Yeah, I'll do it!"

The last two weeks before the show we really had to hustle. My cousin Cassie came over and we spread the cardboards I got from Grandpa out onto the garage floor. We painted a cow, a donkey, and two sheep. Mom helped us cut them out with a one-edged razor. Later, Grandpa made simple stands to nail them to, so they would stand up.

My aunts came up with a great idea; serve hot chocolate and cookies to people when they stopped by to view our nativity. They baked dozens of homemade cookies for the big night.

I printed out "Live Nativity" flyers and placed them on doorknobs all over the neighborhood.

Then disaster hit. Three days before the live nativity, Lucas walked into my bedroom at six-thirty in the morning.

"Remember those mice that chewed away at the organ pipes?" he asked.

His voice was sounding a bit too scratchy.

"Lucas! What's a matter with your voice?" I sat straight up in bed staring in disbelief.

"It sort of hurts," he said, holding his hand over the front of his neck.

I threw back the covers. "No way!"

Mom and Lucas had been practicing their song together all week, he couldn't get sick now! I grabbed Lucas by the hand and marched him to my Mom's bedroom door. I knocked hard.

"Mom, are you in there? Lucas is getting a sore throat!"

"Just a minute!" Within seconds Mom opened the door. She felt my brother's forehead for a temperature.

"How bad does your throat hurt?" she asked him.

"Pretty bad," said Lucas. Then Mom got a flashlight and looked inside his mouth. "Hmmm…looks sore alright, " she said. She decided to take Lucas to have his throat checked for strep. *Whew!* We found out later, no strep throat. We treated him with cherry flavored cough drops, cream of chicken soup, gummy vitamins, and ice cream.

I was off school for a few days, so I was able to help take care of my brother. I read him stories, checked his temperature, fluffed his pillows, and cleaned out his guinea pig's cage. I played Legos. Lots of Legos. I was basically my brother's servant for two days, but I didn't mind. I sort of forgot how much fun it was spending time with my brother. Three days later, Lucas announced his throat didn't hurt. God is good!

On the day of the live nativity, it was thirty-six degrees. The baby goats showed up at 1:00. Grandpa drove metal stakes into the ground to tie the goats to, so they wouldn't wander off. He set up blue yard lights to make our set look like night even in the day. My dog Ella scared the goats. She had to stay in the house. Our dog Tyson was fine. He sat in front of the manger guarding "baby Jesus." The cat ran off and hid.

All the cousins were in costume by 1:30. My aunties and Grandma were hurrying around the kitchen getting hot chocolate and cookie trays together.

We pulled a big bin into position and posted a "Food Donations Here" sign on it. I carefully placed "baby Jesus" in the straw filled manger. Cassie and Olivia, dressed as angels, stood behind the manger holding a glittery banner, which read: "For unto you is born this day in the city of David a Savior who is Christ the Lord."

Kali sat beside the manger, looking positively Mary-like. Jacob stood on the other side, holding a walking stick. The shepherds along with little angels Adeline, Elena and Gemma wandered around the yard keeping watch over the flocks by night. They wouldn't stand in one spot anyway.

A few people from the neighborhood began to gather. I watched as they dropped donations of canned food into the bin. Some people even dropped in money!

I told Mom and Lucas when to start the Silent Night song.

Mom took a spot with her guitar and began to strum, and Lucas began to sing "Silent night, Holy night…" I was so proud of my little brother.

More people showed up—with more food to donate. Cars began to stop, and people got out to watch. An old lady got out some tissues to dry her tears.

"How precious," she said, dabbing her eyes.

"Thanks, sis," Lucas whispered. "This is the best live nativity ever!"

"And you are the best brother ever," I told him.

Miss Jenny came with her aunt and uncle to see the show, before taking the goats home.

"This is fantastic!" she said, looking around.

They listened to Lucas sing, sipping hot chocolate with us. "I can see you put in some real effort into this—I'm so proud of you Jade," she told me.

By 5:30 p.m. we were finished with the show. We had gone through three trays of cookies and five gallons of hot chocolate! Our donation bin was filled to the top with cans and boxes of all sorts of food, plus seventy dollars!

The week after Christmas, everyone who participated in the challenge at school turned in a report on the success of their event. What did I get for leadership, originality, and project success? A+, A+, A+!

Lucas was right. This really was the best live nativity ever!

## Shadow Man

My sister Jenna and I became camp counselors at Camp
Kawishawee last summer. Jenna talked me into it. "Tess,"
she told me, "You need to break out of your shell. Being a
counselor will be an awesome experience!" So I decided to
give it a try.

The first time I stood exasperated in front of a cabin full
of giggling eight-year olds who were supposed to be settling
down for the evening, I wondered if I had made the right
decision. Was I really cut out for this? But life at camp was
about to get a *lot* more complicated than trying to figure that
out.

I looked across an empty field toward the corral. Night
was closing in, but I could still see the head wrangler, John
Bear LaCroix, unsaddling the horses for the night. Good old
John Bear. If it wasn't for him, I may have never figured
out what to do about Gabe. Let me explain what I mean.

My first week at Camp Kawishawee, I was put in
charge of the canteen from two to four o'clock. It was a big
responsibility. Besides snacks and candy for sale, there
were frozen treats and a shop full of camp souvenirs.

It wasn't long before I noticed the camp director's son Gabe didn't pay for what he picked out, like everyone else. I thought that was pretty weird.

"I'll pay later," he told me. He seemed a little shifty—like he was scanning the souvenir shop just to make sure we were the only ones there.

I finally asked him, "How soon is later?"

That's when Gabe told me flat out that he didn't have to pay because his dad ran the camp.

"My dad doesn't have a problem with me taking a candy bar now and then, especially since I sacrificed a better job to work here as a wrangler. "

"That's between you and me," he added. "You know, your sister says you take life way too seriously." Then he walked off with an ice cream bar and a bag of chips!

Other staff must know he does this, I figured. After all, he is the camp director's son. Still it left me speechless. Gabe was eighteen-years-old. He should know better. He acted like he was entitled to whatever he wanted. I didn't want to start anything, so I let it go.

Every weekend at camp we had a special campfire for counselors and staff. Saturday night campfires were an awesome time to break away, re-connect, and re-kindle our faith. Around the fire that night, John Bear told his story first.

"Native people look for wisdom and direction in life like anyone else," he began. "My people pray to Manitou, the Great Spirit who created all things. I sought to know this Creator, and discover him personally. Everywhere I looked pointed me to Jesus. I came to know Jesus as a true warrior, who was not afraid to die for my sins.

Have you ever heard of a warrior who would fight and die so his enemies could be set free? This is what Jesus did for all of us. He won the power to live in our hearts and prepare a place for us in heaven. The natural world could not do this. When I understood these things, I invited him into my life and let Him take control."

I never heard anyone share Jesus the way John Bear did. Then Gabe stood and told how God changed his life at camp over the summer. He said all the right words. He even gave my sister Jenna credit for bringing him "closer to Jesus." But I remembered what he said to me in the canteen. I could still see him walking off with chips and ice cream without paying.

No matter what Gabe said, I couldn't believe him. It was obvious to me that Jesus was not in control of Gabe.

Gabe was! People clapped after he gave his talk, but I just sat there. I had trouble even looking at him, because I knew his dirty little secret.

Later my sister caught up to me as I was walking back to White Pine cabin for the night.

"Tess, wait up. I need to ask you something."

"About what?"

"About your obvious problem with Gabe. What is it?" She grabbed hold of my arm.

"I don't know." I pulled my arm back. "Gabe acts like two different people—it bugs me. I'll see you tomorrow."

"Don't be so quick to judge, Tess. Nobody is perfect."

Jenna's words seemed to hang in the dark and follow me back to my cabin. What did she mean by that? She must realize Gabe is not what he makes himself out to be, or she wouldn't feel the need to say that. I figured he must of put her under his spell.

I couldn't sleep that night. I propped myself up with pillows and tried reading my Bible in the dark with a small flashlight. Finally I fell asleep, but woke up later from a bad dream. It was creepy. I dreamed about a man without a face—just a shadow where there should have been a face.

In the morning, Gabe and Jenna sat together at breakfast. Jenna was laughing and flirting as usual, keeping Gabe gazing in her direction. I guess you could say I was a tad jealous of my sister. She always attracted the cute guys. I looked down at my half-eaten pancakes and sausages and felt a little guilty. Gabe did seem nice enough. Maybe I was over-reacting. Maybe I was being too judgmental. Whatever I was, I was glad Gabe didn't make a visit to the canteen in the afternoon to take something he didn't intend to pay for.

That afternoon I discovered twenty dollars missing from the canteen's cash drawer. I had a sinking feeling about who may have been responsible. I reported the missing money to Ellen, the lead counselor. She said not to worry. She'd check the totals again and let the camp director know if there was a problem.

I stopped by the horse stable during my free time before supper. The other wranglers were gone doing their own thing, but I knew John Bear always hung around the horses. I wanted to know what he thought about Gabe, since they worked with each other so much.

John Bear was polishing a saddle when I walked into the horse barn.

"Hey, Bear," I said.

"Tess – good to see you!"

"A new saddle? It's beautiful!" I told him.

"Yeah – we're getting two new horses this fall. We'll be looking for another wrangler next summer. How about you?"

"Me? A wrangler? Are you serious? I don't have enough experience."

John Bear stopped polishing and set the saddle aside. "You could learn. I've seen how good you handle Blaze and Spirit. Those two are a challenge! They like you."

"Do you think? That would be awesome," I told him.

"I'll put in a good word for you," he said.

"Thanks!"

I hesitated. I knew why I was there. Gabe had caught me in his web, and I needed to talk to somebody about it. He made me feel guilty—like I was protecting him, and it made me angry. I hoped John Bear could give me some good advice.

"Something on your mind?" John Bear asked, pulling out a rusty stool from under the workbench. He offered me a seat. John Bear always seemed to know when something was on your mind. Something big.

I sat. "What do you think about Gabe?" I started. Before he could answer me I added, "I think he tries to get away with stuff—I mean, if you haven't noticed already."

Bear nodded in agreement. "Gabe has his own rules."

I blurted, "But do you think we protect him? I think a lot of people have…"

Just saying that made me feel dizzy, like I was going to slide off the stool sideways.

"What do you mean?" Bear's brow furrowed, and then he looked away.

I knew he knew what I meant.

"Gabe seems to get away with murder around here, just because he's the camp director's son. Think about it."

Bear became thoughtful. "You're right," he said. "I guess I haven't been willing to admit it."

"How do you feel about Gabe taking food out of the canteen whenever he wants, without paying? He says his dad doesn't care if he takes stuff out of the canteen. And the cash register didn't balance today. I counted twenty dollars missing. If Gabe took it, then this has gone too far."

Bear grew thoughtful again. "I hear what you are saying. I haven't taken a hard look at what's been going on with Gabe. Some things are hard to face, like Shadow Man."

"Shadow Man?" I remembered my dream.

"It's a story passed down by the elders of our clan. When a warrior has a vision, it sometimes appears as Shadow Man. You cannot see his face, only a shadow. It means the warrior is afraid or unwilling to face his true enemy." The hair on my arms stood up.

"John Bear, I had a dream last night—I was alone, closing up the canteen, when I noticed a man walking through the souvenir shop without a face—only a shadow where there should have been a face. I looked right at him and asked him in a loud voice, "Who are you?" Then his whole head disappeared. It was creepy. Then I woke up."

Bear stared at me, his eyes darkening.

"Don't you see? I've been unwilling to stand up to Gabe," I told him. "Instead, I let him take over the canteen—protecting him because I was afraid, while he took whatever he wanted. I've been scared and unwilling to let Gabe know how threatened and angry he makes me feel!" My eyes began to burn with tears.

"Hey, don't let this upset you. Listen, I'll talk to him myself. He has no right to make you feel this way. He intimidated a new staffer—this is not your fault."

"So you don't think I'm crazy?"

"Never! Look over there, in the corner."

He pointed to a spider web. "What do you see?"

"A dead beetle caught in a web," I told him.

"Nothing left but the shell," Bear said. "The beetle was the unsuspecting one. Don't call yourself crazy for having your eyes open. It keeps you out of the spider's web."

"John Bear, I should have gone straight to Gabe's dad and asked him about the canteen policy, but I was afraid to. And the more I covered for Gabe, the guiltier I got. If it's alright for Gabe to take stuff out of the canteen, I need to hear it from his dad. Pray for me, would you? I need to do this."

Talking with Gabe's dad the next day was the hardest thing I ever did.

"Gabe's got some issues we are sorting through right now, Tess." His dad also explained Gabe never had the freedom to take stuff out of the canteen without paying for what he took.

"Don't feel guilty about bringing up your concerns, or worried about getting Gabe into trouble," he told me.

I felt sorry for Gabe's dad. He looked embarrassed and sad. He seemed concerned about how the whole situation affected me. It made me wonder why I was so afraid to talk to him about it from the beginning.

I didn't want to tell Jenna I had met with Gabe's dad—not yet. Three days later, rumors began to fly around camp that Gabe was in some sort of trouble. I had to find my sister Jenna, and find her fast. She was alone in Caribou Cabin, curled up on her bunk crying. She looked like she just heard some horrible news.

When I walked in the door she looked at me with swollen, teary eyes. "You were right," she whimpered.

"About what?" I asked.

"About Gabe! He was caught on hidden camera taking money from the cash register in the canteen. Can you believe it?"

My jaw dropped. *Hidden camera? I had no idea.*

"It's such a mess!" Jenna continued, crying in her pillow again, quivering and sobbing.

"Listen," I told her. "At this point all we can do is pray. God is in control of this mess. We've got to pull it together! We have a job to do. We're counselors. The kids need us!"

Jenna sat up. "You're right. I don't know what I'd do without you, Tess."

We hugged and even laughed about the whole crazy turn of events.

Gabe got busted, and I was relieved—relieved because Gabe was forced into the light about himself, and forced to do so something about it. In the meantime, he was dismissed from staff for the rest of the camp season. And I was forced into the light about myself too—forced to confront my own "Shadow Man."

On the last day of camp while waiting to board the bus, I saw John Bear running toward me from the corral. He was wearing a brown-suede cowboy hat. "How do I look?" he hollered.

"Dude!" I yelled, "It's too small!"

"That's because I bought it for you!" He caught up to me, catching his breath. "You'll need it next summer, wrangler. Try it on!"

I sat it on my head—perfect!  "Thanks Bear! I love it!"

On the trip home I leaned back in my seat and daydreamed about Blaze and Spirit, and how I couldn't wait to be a real wrangler. "Next summer is going to totally rock!" I said out loud.

## Shadow Man Part II

## "Thunderstruck"

In a flash, Lightening—the horse I was riding, took a bolt—and I viewed my fall in real time. Me, Tess Larson, flung like a rag-doll between earth and sky and hitting the ground with a sickening thud. I had been bucked! I didn't have time to scream. The world faded into black.

Next, I heard a voice, *"Tess, are you alright?"*

My eyes opened. Gabe, Mitch, and a counselor named Joe were kneeling around me, looking worried. I was the newest wrangler at Kawishawee Bible camp. I shouldn't have ridden Lightening, but Gabe thought I could handle him.

"She wasn't ready for Lightening!" Mitch said to Gabe.

"I didn't say she had to ride him," Gabe said.

All the while, I felt a growing pressure in my chest. I could barely breath! I tried to get up, but the guys told me not to. I started struggling—kicking my legs and throwing my arms around. I managed to gasp,
"No!...I...can't...breath!!" My lungs were killing me. I struggled to my hands and knees, and then it happened. Air sucked in with an uncontrollable *WHOOP*. Mitch helped me

up to my feet, but I ached so bad I could only hunch over, holding my head. Joe grabbed a folding chair out of the barn for me to sit on.

"She got the wind knocked out of her!" he said.

Just then, John Bear came running over. "What happened?"

"She got bucked," said Joe.

"What horse?"

"Lightening."

"She wasn't ready for Lightening—he's not broken in yet! Whose idea was that?"

"Stop arguing, " I interrupted weakly, "I'm alright, everybody just calm down!"

By then the camp nurse appeared and began to check me over. "It doesn't appear like anything is broken, but we're taking you to the hospital in Duluth for a check-up. Your head got a nasty blow. An ambulance is coming."

*Ambulance? Oh brother. This is totally worse than a bad hair day.* A crowd of kids were already beginning to gather and stare.

"I'll go with you," John Bear said.

I smiled weakly and held onto my aching head.

At the hospital, they told me I had a concussion. The doctor told me I couldn't be around the horses for the rest of the summer.

"I don't want you to risk another injury of any kind," he said.

Great. I came to Kawishawee Bible Camp this summer to be a wrangler. I was having a blast. Now what? This stinks. Once the doctor left, I started to cry.

"Tess—it's gonna work out. You won't have to leave camp. They'll find something else for you to do. We only have three weeks left. Besides, you won't have to deal with Gabe."

That sort of made me smile. "How did you know what I was thinking?"

"I don't know. I just figured," said John Bear. He handed me a box of tissues.

"John Bear," I complained, "Why is it whenever I am around Gabe for long enough, something bad happens? I mean, I'm still letting him control me. Like when you left the corral, he talked me into riding Lightening. He kept telling me to shake off my jitters and saddle up and ride him. I didn't feel ready, but Gabe kept making me feel like I should be ready. He's got this way of talking you into things. Why in the world did his dad allow him to work at camp again anyway?" I felt guilty for saying that, but it was true. I flat out didn't trust Gabe. I never thought I was going to have to work with him. Not after last summer, and all the trouble he caused stealing from the canteen. I couldn't believe they let him back!

"I have my own problems," John Bear said. "Gabe and I don't agree on a lot of things. I need to pray for patience and the right heart toward Gabe, otherwise I might be the one leaving."

"No! Don't even think about it! The horsemanship program would fall apart without you! You can't quit!!"

Just then, a nurse stepped in and took my pulse and blood pressure—bad timing! It must have been up a few notches. To my surprise, she knew John Bear.

"Hey there! How are you doing?" she asked.

I could tell he was a little embarrassed. "Ahhh…I'm doing good!"

"Do you know her from somewhere?" I asked later.

"Yeah. I've been here before—I guess she remembers me.

He didn't tell me what he was there for, and I didn't ask.

I spent the night in the hospital for observation. They gave me pain medicine to help me sleep. The next day, my parents showed up and signed papers for my release. I was so happy to see them again.

"You gave us quite a scare," Dad said. "Thank God you didn't break your neck!"

When we got back to camp, my belongings had already been moved to the lodge. The nurse wanted me to sleep upstairs from the main hall. I didn't mind. It was warmer up there, and the bathroom was right across from my room. I was glad my parents wanted to spend the weekend with me to make sure I was well enough to stay for the rest of the summer.

That night, the head cook told me the kitchen needed extra help, so there would be plenty for me to do if I wanted to stay. Of course I said yes!

By week's end I was feeling like my old self again. On Friday night, the staff put on skits. Gabe and Joe made one up called "Buster Joe, the Wild Bronco." Joe, the biggest counselor on staff, was down on his hands and knees under a brown blanket with a paper bag over his "horse head" and a neck tie pinned to the blanket for a tail.

"Who dares ride Buster Joe?" Gabe taunted the kids. "Are you sure you are ready to risk life and limb?"

One by one, the kids were bucked off "Buster Joe" until one rowdy kid managed to pull the whole costume off. The campers thought it was all hilarious, and I joined in the fun, but inside I wasn't laughing. I felt like it was Gabe trying to make me feel stupid for ever riding Lightening—while covering up his own part in the incident.

The next day I volunteered to help my sister Jenna with an activity she was in charge of. Campers were hovering around tables loaded with an assortment of borders, stickers and captions to add to their scrapbooks. Jenna looked trendy with her new reading glasses perched on the tip of her nose and her hair clipped loose in a ponytail. Two French tipped fingernails she stuck on earlier in the day were missing. I spotted one on the floor and handed it back.

"Here's a fingernail you lost."

Jenna sighed, then decided to yank them all off and pitch them the trash.

"I hate these things!" she hissed dramatically.

We laughed. Then while we cut and pasted, she asked me about John Bear.

"Have you noticed how much Bear is away from the horses? Last year you could hardly pull him away, now it seems he's gone half the time. That's not like John Bear."

"He said he has appointments. I didn't ask for what. I didn't think it was any of my business."

Our conversation drew the attention of Trina, a camper.

"Is John Bear alright?"

"Yes, he's fine—how's that scrapbook coming?" Jenna asked, moving over toward Trina.

That got me thinking. Maybe something really was wrong with John Bear. I put two and two together—his sudden tired spells, the nurse who remembered him; Bear not seeming like his old self anymore. Something was definitely wrong. I had to find out what it was.

Before reporting back for kitchen duty, I walked over to John Bear's cabin and knocked. He shuffled to the screen door and looked out.

"Tess—what is it?"

"Hey—uhhh...I was wondering...Can we hike to Apostle Rock once I finish kitchen chores tonight? Nothing earth shattering or anything..."

"Yeah...sure....is there something you want to talk about?"

I paused. "Yeah….just…well everything…Meet me at the lodge around seven?"

"Sure…"

"Thanks Bear. I gotta go. See you later."

"Yeah sure. See ya."

Apostle Rock stands on top of the highest bluff that surrounds Kawishawee Bible camp. It juts up under a stand of twelve Red Pines. You can view the whole camp from up there. It's big and awesome and sort of iconic. Everyone knows if you want to get away to think and pray, or talk about something important – you take a hike to the Rock.

When we got there, we discovered Gabe and a sixteen-year old junior counselor named Gabby. They basically have the same name—Gabriel and Gabriella, but neither of them were looking too angelic at the time, partly because Gabby was a junior counselor, and too young to be hiking up to the Rock or anywhere else with Gabe, and partly because Gabe was basically on probation after last summer's incident in the canteen.

"Gabby lost her glasses and I was helping her find them," said Gabe.

Gabby pulled out a pair of glasses from her pocket and agreed. "Yeah…*whew*! I finally found them."

"What are you two doing?" Gabe asked us. "Going on a vision quest?"

"We came here to talk," John Bear said, picking up on Gabe's sarcasm.

"Sure you are. C'mon Gabby, let's go."

They turned and hiked back down the trail toward camp. Before they were out of sight, Gabby turned and waved goodbye. I waved back. She was such a sweet girl, just like Jenna, and she was falling under Gabe's spell. I hoped there was still time to rescue her from total entrapment.

I reminded myself that Gabe and Gabby were not the reason I came to the Rock, and I didn't want to waste any time getting to the point of why I came. We sat down and I jumped in.

"Bear, remember last summer at camp when you asked me what was on my mind? Well…now I am asking you the same thing. Something is wrong. Can we talk?"

John Bear hesitated. "We can talk, but it's just between you and me." I guess he knew what I wanted to know.

He waited a few more moments, then continued. "Tess…I'm not well."

"What do you mean?"

"I have a sickness…in my liver …it's chronic."

"What is it?"

"A virus. I have the worst kind… I may have to live with it—permanently."

"So that's where you go every Tuesday? To the hospital?"

"Yes. I drive in every week for an injection, and I'm taking a pill twice a day. It might get rid of the virus, and it might not."

"How did you get it?"

"A tattoo. The guy who ran the shop reused tattoo needles on people. Some people got sick. I was one of them. A couple years later, I started showing symptoms. Stupid isn't it? All because I wanted an eagle on my shoulder— now I wish I would have never gotten it."

I didn't know what to say. "Am I the only person at camp that knows about this?"

"The director knows, and the nurse, and a few others."

"What about next year? You're coming back, aren't you?"

"I don't know, Tess. If I don't get rid of this I might be too big of a risk."

"John Bear, I'll pray you'll be healed. You're the best wrangler we ever had!  We don't want you to have to go."

"Thanks Tess. I know God's in charge. We just need to trust Him. I guess we better head back."

The week went south after that. Gabe told Mitch he thought John Bear and I were spending more time in the barn grooming horses than was appropriate. What a joke! And if John Bear and I were spotted together on the campgrounds, Gabby's friends would whisper and stare. It was so lame.

I told John Bear I had it with Gabe. "Gabe's spreading rumors, and Gabby is under his spell, just like Jenna was last summer. Maybe Jenna and I can get her talking. Maybe the two of us can pull her out of his web," I told him.

Jenna and I got our chance on the beach during free time. It was perfect! I had the day off—my whole afternoon was basically free. We spread our beach towels out on either side of Gabby while she tanned. She looked up and was surprised to be surrounded by the Larson girls. I mean, she couldn't exactly escape us—we were there on a mission.

"You don't mind if we tan with you, do you?" we asked.

"Ahh… sure…whatever…sunscreen anyone?" She handed us a tube of SPF 30.

"Thanks!" We smoothed some on. After about five minutes of girl talk, it was time to get serious.

"Gabby, you know Gabe and I hung out all last summer, right?" Jenna started.

"Yeah," Gabby said—then laughed. "Gabe said you weren't his type."

"No, I'm definitely not. I guess what Tess and I want you to know is…well…we don't believe you are either—if you think you ever might be that is."

*Uhh Oh. That didn't sound so good.*

"What are you trying to say? There is nothing going on between me and Gabe," said Gabby.

I could see we were getting nowhere fast.

"I think what Jenna is trying to say," I interrupted "Is you deserve the best experience you can have at camp, and if Gabe's making you feel pressured, that's a problem. Don't protect him just because he's the camp director's son."

Gabby stood to her feet. "You know, you two are beginning to sound like my parents. Look, everything is cool. Nothing horrible is happening. Stop worrying! Anyway, I think I'm getting burnt. I better get going."

Gabby shook out her beach towel and grabbed her bag. "See you later." Sand flew onto us as she tromped off.

Jenna and I looked at each other feeling a little sheepish. Maybe we were jumping to conclusions. At any rate, we hoped we said something right.

Everything came to a head the last week of camp. We had a youth rally in the chapel. Dex Davison and his wife Sophia were the closing speakers. They were awesome. Jenna and I hoped that somehow God would help Gabby know we were on her side and trying to help.

Dex talked about the meaning of commitment and how important it was to guard our hearts so we could be healthy and happy, the way God intended for us to be. He invited anyone to stay after the rally if they wanted to talk to him, or Sophia, or a counselor about anything. Jenna and I were sitting in the front pew—and Gabby came and sat down next to us.

"We need to talk," she announced. Gabe followed her, but I reminded him of the chapel code—guys counsel guys and girls counsel girls. Gabby couldn't seem to make one move without Gabe hovering over her like a helicopter! He went and sat down on the other side of the chapel, but didn't look too happy about it.

Gabby began, "Thanks guys. What you said makes sense. I mean, you were totally right. Gabe is too old for me and...well, I'd like you to pray for me."

At that point, Sophie came over. "Hey girls—mind if I join you?"

She told us how she once decided to break off an unhealthy relationship in order to put Jesus first in her life.

Gabby announced, "I'm definitely ready to do that!"

Sophie shared some bible promises, and then we all prayed. In fact, we all asked Jesus to take total control of our lives and make us into the followers that He wanted us to be.

Afterwards, I asked Sophie and the girls to pray for John Bear. "He is going through a lot right now."

Then Gabby dropped a bombshell. She asked us all to pray for Gabe.

My thoughts boomeranged. *What? We're not praying for Gabe. He's watching us like a hawk from the other side of the chapel. Besides, I've had it with his schemes! Ever since last summer he's had it in for me. He treats people like pawns, and acts like he is entitled to anything. I doubt if he will ever change. He'll always be a two-faced, manipulative, impossible-to-trust "Shadow Man." How in the world could I ever seriously pray for Gabe?*

All these thoughts shot into my head like a hurricane. Then I heard words coming out of my mouth from some impossible place saying,

"Yeah, you're right, I guess we should pray for Gabe."

*What?? What are you talking about?* My brain was silently screaming, *What are these crazy words jumping off the end of my tongue?* The fact is, I didn't really want to pray for Gabe. At the same time I knew God was putting his finger on a big problem in my life, and I had thunder-struck written all over me.

"Tess... is something wrong?" Sophie asked.

Our eyes met.

"Oh, I...I have some issues with Gabe I need to deal with," I said blankly. "I guess maybe I'm the one who needs prayer, before I can pray for him."

Gabby and Jenna looked at me and began to half-laugh and half-cry at the same time. They knew how mad and crazy Gabe could make you feel. We locked arms, bowed our heads, and prayed for each other, for the camp, for John Bear, and yes, for Gabe. Afterwards, I looked across the chapel and noticed he was gone. I guess he got tired of waiting and watching.

That night I turned my hard feelings toward Gabe over to the Lord, and received God's forgiveness. It would still be a daily challenge, not letting Gabe get under my skin, but I also knew God's promise: *"I can do all things through Christ who strengthens me."*

There are circumstances in life I can never change—like I can't change the fact that John Bear got sick from getting a tattoo. And I can't change people. Only God can do that. But with Jesus in my heart, I can let allow God to change me. That's always the best place to start.

# Sophia and the Sacred Spaces

**(Sophia tells the story of how she met Dex, and Jesus.)**

"Sometimes we are changed forever through one singular encounter. It happened to me on a whitewater trip in May. I was seventeen, and the only girl I knew that paddled whitewater with her dad every spring.

I was standing on a boat landing watching the Snake River forge downstream over a low head dam. Dad was in the parking area unloading our canoe. He had arranged a shuttle with a co-worker named Dave Davison, about to arrive with his son Dex any minute. I had never met them.

It was my first canoe trip of the season, and my adrenaline was pumped. I knew the Snake River was tricky in low water and risky in high. I also knew one ill stroke of the paddle and we'd be swimming either way.

I sensed someone standing behind me, and turned to look. It was a guy, maybe eighteen or so, holding his arms across his chest.

"What do think of the river?" he asked.

"Pushy," I said. "You must be..."

"Dave's son," he answered. "This is our first time on the Snake. Have you paddled it before?"

"Three times. You guys can rescue us when we wipe out in the rapids," I said.

"I'm all over it. By the way, my name is Dex."

"I'm Sophie. You guys are planning to have lunch with us, right? We brought extra food and homemade cookies. Trust me, they're good."

"That's cool. We'll watch out for you guys on the water. We wouldn't want the food to get wet."

I remembered those words later as Dad and I paddled through rough rapids, shooting past boulders and cutting through two-foot waves. I looked behind us to see if I could spot Dex and his dad's purple-and-green kayaks.

About one hour into the trip, I drew in my paddle to avoid a boulder. I wasn't quick enough, and we hit – dead on. Our boat took a sideways twist and capsized.

Dad and I were bouncing in our life jackets like two red bobbers in a washing machine when Dex and his dad caught up to us.

The river spun us around a curve and spit us toward a small eddy near the bank. Dex helped steer us toward shore so we could pull ourselves out of the river. Dad held onto his paddle, but mine was headed downstream somewhere. I rescued the sealed cooler with our lunch instead.

"It's a good thing you grabbed the food," Dex told me, "Otherwise you two would still be swimming!"

"Very funny," I told him. Dad and I climbed up the bank to safety.

"You'll need these," Dex said, throwing us a thick towel to dry with, and two dry shirts.

While dad and I rubbed the water out of our wetsuits, Dex and his dad took off downstream and located our boat, pulling it out of a snag. As for the lost paddle, Dex had an extra one strapped to his kayak just in case of a mishap. I hoped to find mine floating downstream later on.

After all the excitement was over, we decided to take a lunch break. Dex and I walked down to the river's edge and sat down on a log.

"So, do you go kayaking a lot?" I asked.

"Yeah, this is the best time of the year."

"Going to school?"

"I'm a junior in college. And you?"

"I'm graduating high school the end of the month. No definite plans. What are you going to do?"

"Be a youth pastor," he told me. Then he paused and added, "Surprised?"

"Well, a little. You don't seem like..."

"...the type?" He finished my sentence before I could.

"Well, maybe you do—hey seriously, I think it's great. So...your mission in life is kids! That's cool."

While I stuffed myself with cookies, Dex talked about his faith in God as if I were an old friend. I was skeptical, but interested.

"Reaching kids won't be easy," I told him. "Kids think people like you are a little freaky."

"Yeah, some kids are hard to reach, but some are ready to listen. You know, everybody has a sacred space—a space worth protecting from the enemy, a space meant for God. That's the message I want to bring to kids."

"A sacred space?" I asked. "If there's anything sacred in this world, you won't find it in the average high school kid these days." I looked over my shoulder at Dad and Dave. This conversation was getting a little intense.

Dex continued to explain, "Our eyes, our ears, our whole bodies can be bridgeheads for the enemy to cross over and mess up our lives, you know what I'm saying? Whatever keeps us from doing God's will is the enemy. We need to guard the gates. We need Jesus."

"Right," I said, taking a swig of diet pop.

I had to create a detour in this conversation. I wasn't sure where Dex was taking me, but I didn't think I was ready to go there. I tried another angle to deflect what he was saying. I didn't want God prying into my life in the form of Dex. I was actually beginning to feel a little annoyed.

"I suppose if we were all like you—all into God and stuff, it would be easy to guard the gates," I said. "But things happen to kids who aren't looking for trouble. Not every kid has a neat bridge to cross over into sainthood, if that's what you're talking about. It's like we've been shoved into this river, and it is swarming with alligators. Some of us make it across, and some of us don't. Some of us get so messed up it's too late to guard the gates. How can God expect us not to mess up, and then turn around and condemn us when we do?"

Dex looked downstream toward the rapids.

*He might make a great date if he wasn't so religious,* I thought. Now I only wanted to toss his tee-shirt back, but of course I didn't. I was about to get up and walk away, when he spoke up.

"Sophie – lots of kids are messed up and hurting these days. Jesus said he didn't come here to condemn us, but to save us. The world is a scary place, but His power is available to make us into whatever he wants us to be. We were a part of his plan, even before we knew how to believe. When Christ died, we were blood bought."

*Blood bought? What was that supposed to mean?* Apparently Dex was trying to ignite the same faith in me that he had, but so far it wasn't working.

"You're blood bought," I told him, "And other nice people like you. Thanks, but the rest of us just might be out of luck."

I picked up my leftovers and headed back up the bank. I felt bad for saying that, and I had to admit Dex appeared to really care about me. He obviously wasn't interested in putting words in my mouth. I thought of Dad and his friend Dave. Dad had been visiting Dave's church lately. I began to suspect Dad had planned this whole thing. Pretty sneaky, old dad.

For the next few days, I kept thinking about our conversation on the Snake. Dex texted scripture verses to me that I could look up.

*II Corinthians 5:15-21* really stood out, especially verse 15, *"...He died for all, that they who live should henceforth not live unto themselves, but unto Him who died for them and rose again."*

Slowly I began to realize the ball was in my court. I began to envision what it would mean if I truly was blood-bought. If I was blood-bought, then everything would have to change. It would mean giving God what rightfully belonged to him—namely, my heart. It would mean stopping the argument with God I cherished, because if His power was available for me to live the way he wanted me to, what was I mad about? I was beating the air. The fog in my head was beginning to lift.

I suddenly realized that not believing Christ had bought me for Himself, enabled me to live for myself, without regard to His great work for me. It was the main roadblock—the chief sin. It shut Jesus out of my life. God was waking me up out of a dead sleep. I knew that if I turned away from Him at this point, I might never be inclined to hear His voice again.

So I believed. Yes—I was blood-bought—Jesus died and rose again to live His life in me. "Lord Jesus, forgive me for the unbelief that has shut You out of my life for so long," I prayed. "Fill me with your Holy Spirit. Make me into the person you want me to be, in your Name I pray, Amen."

Ten years later, I look out from a small podium into a sea of teenage faces. In an instant, I remember. I was once one of those faces – hopeful and despairing, daring and afraid, full of ideals, but caving into the pressure of being someone I didn't really want to be. I tap my microphone to make sure it's on. "Guys and girls, my name is Sophia Davison. Sometimes we are changed forever through one singular encounter. It happened to me ten years ago on a whitewater trip in May..."

## The Rest of Amos

'A dark foreboding ushered me to sleep last night,' Colette wrote. 'I had another dream about water. It rose fast, and went no place that I could see, but was everywhere. It rose around my feet inside a shabby little house I'd never seen, climbing the walls to an attic.'

Colette remained focused, her pen feverish as she continued to write:

'I ran up some stairs and found a spot where I could lay between the rafters. A warm breeze was blowing through an open window. The air smelled sweet and swollen, the way it does before a storm—the kind of air that just might sweep you up if you're not lucky. I sat up and looked out the open window.

In an instant, I was standing alongside a grassy bank, staring at a floating bed upon the water. Old Amos lay upon the bed. His wooly hair was matted to the pillow. His eyes were fixed on something—I couldn't tell what. His skin looked taut and gray. Amos floated on the restless water tired and alone, and I stood silent and powerless—afraid to walk out and pull him back. Instead I turned around and looked away. When I turned back to look again, the water began to shimmer. It shimmered like crystal and sapphire—

beautiful and haunting. While I stood watching, a hole began to form beside the floating bed, and the shimmering water began to rush in. Where the water went, I couldn't tell. Once more, I turned away. When I turned to look again, old Amos was gone.'

Colette stopped writing. She felt bound up, and uneasy. She folded the paper in half, and in half again, and buried the dream between the pages of a book inside the nightstand. After a predictable round of visits and phone calls, Colette lay quiet in the dark, pretending to be asleep as the nursing staff slipped in and out, making their rounds. Perhaps tonight, there would be no dreams. Colette comforted herself with the thought.

Nine o'clock the next morning, Colette washed her face and looked intently in the bathroom mirror. Her fragile hair was just beginning to fill in. She pulled a knit cap over a scar that wrapped around her head like a jagged crown. To Colette, it was a badge of dishonor. Her body had become her enemy, and she didn't know why. She made her way through the halls of Mercy Hospital to room 425.

Short and thin, and wrapped in a pink chenille robe, Colette appeared in the doorway, unannounced.

"Hello Amos, do you mind if I visit?" she inquired.

"Colette! No mind at all – come on in! How you doing, girl?" he asked.

"I'm doing much better. How are you?"

"Oh fine, jus' fine. Pull up a chair! How long you staying here?"

Colette explained, "I'm going through another round of tests this week. I'll probably have more treatments…and my hair was just starting to come back!"

She tugged on her cap, and slouched into a chair.

"No mind, you beautiful! You still havin' those crazy water dreams?" Amos asked.

A flash rippled through Colette's veins. Funny he should ask.

"Oh, now and then," Colette said, looking away as she spoke.

She knew Amos was referring to their last therapy session for hospital patients dealing with terminal illness. She had talked about her water dreams. "Dr. Belding told me to write them down. He thinks it will help."

Amos thought a few moments, "Hmmm…maybe so. Maybe your dreams tellin' you something.' Maybe they tellin' you somethin' big is bindin' you up."

Colette grew thoughtful, then shifted in her chair. "I don't know..."

Suddenly she blurted "Are you afraid of dying?" All at once the room appeared detached—surreal. She couldn't believe she asked someone she barely knew such a personal question.

"Dying?" Amos asked. "Who you askin' girl? No, I ain't afraid."

He paused, leaned toward her and said, "I dreamed about water once."

"Really? What did you dream?"

Colette appeared cool, but felt her heart pounding in her chest.

"Well," Amos continued, "It was nothin' like anything I ever dreamed. I dreamed about heaven, and King Jesus sittin' on a throne. And a river flowed out from underneath that throne—a shiny river of life. Ain't no telling where that shiny river comes from or where it goes. I jus' know that river rose up and swallowed up all my troubles. Everything I ever done wrong, and everything I never done right. It jus' opened up its big old mouth and swallowed 'em up whole."

"Swallowed 'em up whole," Colette repeated softly.

"What's that you say?" Amos asked.

"Oh, nothing. I was just thinking—it was nothing."
Colette felt as if her thoughts were turning inside out.

"And so I ain't afraid of dying," Amos continued. "I
jus' fix my eyes on Jesus, and know I'll be fine. I rest my
soul, and let King Jesus do what he do." Amos leaned his
head back on his pillow. He closed his eyes as if resting in
another place.

Colette lifted her eyes to a small crucifix hanging on the
wall. *King Jesus—dying for me* she thought. *For everything
I ever did wrong, and everything I never did right. He wore
a jagged crown around his head. He knew me. Forgive me
Lord for everything I ever did wrong, and everything I
never did right.*

"I see," she told Amos. "Death doesn't have to be
scary."

A nurse stepped into the room. "Mr. Tombs, I'm here
to wheel you down to physical therapy. Dr. Johnson wants
you up and dancing by Valentine's Day."

She turned to Colette, "Hello, Colette! You must be
feeling better now."

"I am. Thanks." Colette turned to Amos. "Would you
mind if I come again?"

"No mind, no mind at all. Stop in any time!"

"I will," Colette promised. "I'll stop by again soon."

On a muggy afternoon in August, a man with a cane stepped off the elevator outside Unit D at Mercy Hospital. He made his way past the nurse's station and on to room 425. A nurse's aide was adjusting Colette's pillows as the old man tucked his cane into a corner.

The man approached her bedside, taking her hand, watching her eyes. At four o'clock, Dr. Belding stopped in to pay a visit.

"Hello, Mr. Tombs," he said in a hushed tone, "It's good you to see you again."

The doctor looked down on Colette. "How is she?"

Amos thought a moment. "She's floatin,' Doc.' She's floatin' somewhere between here and there. But she's resting. She's resting jus' fine."

Later, as family gathered around Colette's beside, Amos slipped away and walked outside to catch a bus. The air smelled sweet and swollen, the way it does before a storm—*the kind of air that just might sweep you up,* the old man thought. *But no mind about that—she's safe. Yes sir, she's safe with King Jesus.*

# The Tale of Timorous

## And How He Found His New Name

Once upon eternity, in a place that was and is, and is to come, a curious young man frail of temper, and prone to scrupulosity made his dwelling in a simple cottage. His name was Timorous. He lived near a pleasant vineyard in the beautiful city of Zion—a city filled with the bounty of a great and glorious King.

Timorous lived alone, not because he disliked the company of people, but because it gave him time to think – which is the one thing Timorous loved to do. The problem was, Timorous would often think too long on a particular matter, until it became impossible for him to understand what the real matter was, which is often the case with such scrupulous souls. Yet, the gracious King who ruled in Zion, whose name was Wonderful [1] loved Timorous in spite of who he was, and gave him a new name, a true name, which Timorous was destined to discover. [2]

Now concerning this King, I suppose even the world itself could not contain all the books that should be written of him, [3] for the King himself, at a predetermined time in a foreign land, for the joy that was set before him [4] fulfilled a Law no one beside himself could keep. As a result, all who belonged to Him were redeemed from the curse of that Law at the price of the King's own blood.[5] Now the people of Zion were free to serve him forever under a New Law [6] – the Law of Love.[7]

Yet still, there remained a certain peril. Cruel rulers of darkness would seek to infiltrate the beautiful kingdom. Their mission: to destroy all citizens loyal to the King and his New Law. For this reason, it was needful the King call for his loyal scribes to gather around his throne.

"Write in the great Book," he charged. "Rulers of darkness [8] will seek to reclaim all that I have won. Warn my citizens, they must prepare for a coming battle."

Now it was the King's delight to enlist the most unlikely rank of castoff rabble one might ever imagine to enter into his service.[9] People like Timorous. Timorous Warywart to be exact. Friends would often cajole poor Timorous and call him "Timorous Worrywart," to which Timorous would always protest and say, "I am not a worrywart, I am a Warywart! There is a difference you know!"

Actually, there was not much difference at all. For on any given day, Timorous could be heard saying things like "I'm just not sure about that," or "I'm really wary about that," while every loose worrywart from one side of his brain would wiggle its way back to the other. Which made Timorous exactly who he was – an anxious, timorous, double-minded sort of man.[10] No wonder he wavered from one opinion to the next! Which is to say, why on earth would the King choose Timorous?

Now it was known throughout the land, that all citizens great and small were required to take preparations at the King's Grace-fort. At the fort they were shown from the King's great Book what to do under enemy attack, how to fight against the powers of darkness, and how to protect themselves with various pieces of the King's own armor.[11] Each recruit received a copy of the great Book, in which were written all of the King's commandments, promises, and instructions for putting on His armor. Every possible provision was included to enable the recruits to win their battles.[12]

With all this provision, some of the recruits began to feel dauntless, even invincible—except for Timorous. He listened quietly as the other soldiers rallied in their boastings.

"This is our final night of preparations. There is no reason why we can't relax, and take our ease," said a soldier called Slack.

"You're right," boasted another man called Presumption.

Slack and Presumption decided to spend the evening throwing dice with a recruit named Carnal Confidence. Wanting to appear as brave and confident as Slack and the others, Timorous tucked the King's great Book and the King's own armor under his cot, and put his worrywarts to rest. But he forgot one crucial bit of advice: The enemy strikes when you least expect him.

Later that night while the recruits lay sleeping, a damp fog rolled into the camp, and the starless night became eerie and black. Suddenly a cry rang out!

"Rulers of darkness! Take cover!" [13]

At once fiery darts began to tear through the tent. Timorous woke up and rolled to the floor, covering his head with his hands. Within seconds, the whole camp was set into a flaming fit. Waves of burning barbs struck the unarmed. Confusion reigned. Some ran. Others took cover.

Timorous grabbed as much armor as he could possibly hold and burst out of the tent, running east into the fog towards the Forest of Entangle. Barely reaching the woods, he was pierced by a flaming dart. Tearing it from his leg, he pushed his way through a thick bramble and agonizing, collapsed near a dirt road. Every piece of armor was lost on the run—except for the King's own shield.[14]

After catching his breath, Timorous struggled back to his feet and looked beyond the thicket, past the fog and over the open field. The fort was ablaze.

*Now what do I do?* he asked himself. *Cross the field and return to the fort?* Wounded and barely able to hold onto the King's shield, he doubted whether he should cross the open field and return to the Grace-Fort. After much wavering, Timorous decided he had better turn back and take the path into the Forest of Entangle.[15] He hoped it would lead him to the King's Highway and back to the city of Zion.

As he stood trembling and doubtful on the edge of the forest, Timorous began to think, *Would that I was willing to die a free man instead of skulking on the edge of this forest, the prisoner of a wounded leg.* The more he considered his case, the more Timorous despised his condition.[16] He ripped the sleeve from his shirt and tied it around his wounded leg. Dazed and disheartened, he lay beside the tangled brush waiting for the daystar to appear.[17]

At break of day, Timorous limped along the path into the forest until he saw two flickering lights shining through the trees, barely visible. Breaking into a large opening in the forest, he discovered the flickering lights were two lit torches attached to either side of a crude portal leading to a great stone house. Hoping to find some refreshment and a soothing balm for his wounded leg, his hopes rallied.

Timorous approached the portal cautiously, removing one of the torches from within its sheath. Holding it before him,[18] he slowly walked into the entrance of the crude portal. The torch revealed the walls were rough and loosely formed, appearing to be a mixture of clay and straw. The portal supported two long tablets of stone overhead, engraved with an ancient writ. Ahead of him, stood an iron gate guarding the door to the great stone house.

Inching forward, Timorous reached for the handle of the iron gate, when immediately he felt the ground beneath him quake. The quake increased to a dangerous tremor. He looked up and saw the stone tablets begin to shift, while the walls on either side begin to crack. Timorous swung around and ran, stumbling out of the portal amid the dust of falling debris.

Upon replacing the torch into its sheath, the rumbling abruptly stopped, and the portal was spared a disastrous collapse. Then Timorous was enlightened.[19] He understood that the portal was unable to bear the weight of the two stone tablets, being cursed of its own corruption. Trusting in the portal would only lead to a false hope,[20] and unless grace should intervene,[21] sudden destruction would fall upon all those unwilling to escape its determined doom. For once in his life, Timorous was glad he had come from a family of anxious Warywarts, who labored long in thought, but knew when to run.

Still curious, Timorous walked around to the side of the house and found an open window, just low enough to look inside. *The house is occupied,* he surmised, *and I do so long for a drink of cool water.*[22] Cautiously, he peered through the window into a dimly lit room. There he saw a tired old woman, carrying a heavy sack upon her back, which made her bow and groan.[23] Her bony fingers held tightly onto crude utensils. With these tools she cooked on an iron grill for a churlish young man sitting on a stone seat. He appeared to be her son.

The man barked demands at the old woman, calling her names and hurling sore insults. Timorous marveled that the more she fed him, the more demanding he became, yet he lifted not one finger to lift off her burden, or assist her in any way.[24] Upon closer examination, Timorous observed a chain clamped around the ankle of the old woman's foot, and the chain led to the stone seat.

*This is no place for a drink of water, or a soothing balm for my stinking wound* [25] Timorous chided himself as he slipped away from the open window. He could see the old woman was a slave, and her son was a self-serving cad. Neither could not give him a drink, nor aid his wound at any cost. Timorous cast out all hope for himself from the bondwoman and her son, and limped back to the path from which he came.[26] No sooner had he returned, when he stumbled over a block of wood, and crumpled to the ground, wincing in pain. "Oh that the way had been cleared," he moaned [27] "So I may not have stumbled—yet will I seek a straight path for my feet, so that which is lame will not be turned out of the way".[28] Then Timorous fell asleep.

An hour or so passed, when a wind began to blow across his fevered brow. He began to stir. When he opened his eyes, a man was kneeling beside him, holding the King's great Book.

"Sir!" said Timorous, "Has the King called Wonderful sent you? I am in an awful state as you can see."

"Indeed, the King has sent me," said the man. "I am a minister, sent forth to minister to those who are the heirs of His kingdom".[29] "I was sent to bring you the King's great Book, to recover your armor, and to point you to the King's Highway."

Timorous sat up and saw the King's whole armor lying on the ground beside him. He perceived he spoke not to a man, but to an angel sent from Zion.

"The King's own armor! Thank you sir!" Timorous exclaimed.

"If you had exercised the King's shield as instructed in His great Book, you could have recovered the rest of his armor at any time," the angel said. He held out the great Book, and where the pages opened to he read: *"Let us draw near with a true heart, in full assurance of faith, having our hearts sprinkled from an evil conscience, and our bodies washed with pure water. Let us hold fast the profession of our faith without wavering, for He is faithful that promised,"* (Hebrews 10:22-23KJV).

Timorous looked into the angel's eyes, and saw as it were a holy fire. At once he knew why he was wounded and wandering in the Forest of Entangle. He had failed to take up and use the Shield of Faith. He had looked to his own strength,[30] failing to remember that in himself he was powerless.[31] He had failed to watch and pray.[32] He slept while the great Book and the King's own armor were hidden under his bed.[33] He forgot all of God's benefits.[34] Acknowledging these failings, Timorous began to tremble.

The angel spoke solemnly, "Timorous, why did you run for cover to the Forest of Entangle? Know this, oh ye of little faith, it is the King himself who has preserved you. Were it not for the King's own choosing [35] you would have opened the iron gate that lets men in, but lets no man out. Remember the bond-woman."

When Timorous recalled the cruel scene he cried out,

"Oh wretched man that I am! Who shall deliver me from the body of this death? I thank my sovereign King who by grace has not justly condemned me!" [36] Thus, being convinced of his own wretchedness, Timorous wept and made confession.[37]

After a time, the angel lifted Timorous to his feet and spoke kindly. "Take courage friend. Question not whether one so timorous as yourself should have the right to wear the King's own armor. The King has won your right. Forget those things which are behind, and press on toward the things which are before." (38)

The angel continued to exhort from the great Book, and the more Timorous listened, the stronger in faith he became. Soon he realized his hunger and his thirst were gone.(39) "Remove the cloth from around your leg," the angel instructed. Timorous loosened and unwound the cloth. "The wound... It's gone!" he marveled.

The angel smiled, and looked toward heaven. "I must depart," he said. "Have faith in God." (40) *Be strong and of good courage, be not afraid, neither be thou dismayed, for the Lord thy God is with thee, whithersoever thou goest" (Joshua 1:9 KJV).*

"Return to Zion by way of the Kings highway. As long as you remain on the Highway you will be safe. No lion shall devour you there, nor any ravenous beast. For only the redeemed shall walk thereon." (41) Then as suddenly as he appeared, the angel vanished.

Timorous was alone, but not alone. He felt the power of the King all around him. He returned to the Book and began to read, *"Wherefore, take unto you the whole armor of God, that ye may be able to withstand in the evil day, and having done all, to stand," (Ephesians 6:13 KJV).*

Following the instructions in the King's great book, Timorous gird his loins with Truth, and covered himself with the breastplate of righteousness.[42] On his feet he fastened the gospel of peace.[43] On his head he wore the helmet of salvation.[44]

Then holding Sword of the Spirit [45] in one hand, and the Shield of Faith [46] in the other, Timorous walked the dirt path back to the King's highway going in the strength of the Lord of lords and King of kings.[47]

A steep ravine ran along the length of the path between the great stone house and the King's Highway. It was a fearsome chasm known by all to emit unearthly howls, hissings, and ungodly snarls from within its depths.

*"Be strong and of good courage,"* Timorous reminded himself as he made his way forward, trying not to look down into the abyss. No sooner had he quoted these words, than a peculiar low-pitched gnarl rose from the pit. Timorous knew beyond all doubt what he was hearing. It was the gnarl of the roaring lion known to lurk about "...seeking those for whom he may devour."[48]

Timorous halted. Should he go forward or backward? To run away in fear risked ruin. He remembered his former skullduggery on the edge of the Forest of Entangle; how he had lost nearly all the King's armor, and wished he had died a free man instead of skulking around with a wounded leg. *Not again!* thought Timorous.

*The King of kings and Lord of lords is with me wherever I go,* he reminded himself. *The angel assured me the beast would not be allowed to tread upon the King's Highway. Therefore, as long as I remain there, his harm is limited to taunt, scare, and discourage me in the Way only.*

Timorous turned to face the ravine. Then, holding up the Sword of the King's great Book in one hand, and the Shield of Faith in the other, he lifted up his voice and called upon the Name of the Lord.[49] The beast's ungodly roar pummeled the air. Timorous could smell the stench of the scabby fiend, and feel the blast of its roar rattle his armor, but still he stood firm.

The lion continued to spit and snarl, but he was bound by the force of the King's own name and the words in the Book. Therefore, seeing he was checked, the beast changed his tact and spoke cunningly and with craft. "My, how the wretched Timorous looks all glorious today—who thinks he owns the right to wear the King's array! Who do you think you are Timorous Warywart?" he mocked.

"I am a man seeking Zion, and of the King's redeemed, and what I think I am this day is more important than I ever dreamed! The King appointed me a name for which I have no merit of my own to bear. And for the threat of you my foe, His armor I am obliged to wear.

My name, devouring beast, is no more Timorous—it is True Heart—and a Christian I am not ashamed to be, for I have drawn near to the King who saves, and the King has drawn near to me!" [50]

At this confession, the beast hissed, and spit, and slowly skulked away, knowing he had lost the game. So ends the tale of Timorous, and how he found his new name.

## Scripture References for The Tale of Timorous

Isaiah 9:6 [1]  Revelation 2:17 [2]  John 21:25b [3]  Hebrews 2:2 [4]  Galatians 3:13 [5]  Romans 8:2 [6]  John 13:34 [7] Ephesians 6:12 [8]  1 Corinthians 1:27-29 [9]  James 1:8 [10] Ephesians 6:13 [11]  II Peter 1:3-4 [12]  Ephesians 6:12 [13] Ephesians 6:16 [14]  Galatians 5:1 [15]  Romans 7:24 [16] II Peter 1:19 [17]  Matthew 6:23 [18]  II Samuel 22:29 [19] Job 8:13-15 [20]  Ephesians 2:8 [21]  John 7:37 [22]  Psalm 38:4 [23]  Matthew 23:2-4 [24]  Psalm 38:5 [25]  Galatians 4:30-31 [26]  Isaiah 57:14 [27]  Hebrews 12:12-13 [28] Hebrews 1:14 [29]  Galatians 3:3 [30]  John 15:5 [31] Matthew 26:41[32]  I Thess. 5:6-8 [33]  Psalm 103:2-3 [34] John 15:16 [35]  Romans 7:24, 8:1 [36]  John 1:9 [37] Philippians 3:13 [38]  Matthew 5:6 [39]  Mark 11:22 [40]  Isaiah 35:8-10 [41]  Ephesians 6:14 [42]  Ephesians 6:15 [43] Ephesians 6:17 [44]  Ephesians 6:17 [45]  Ephesians 6:16 [46] Psalm 71:16 [47]  1 Peter 5:8 [48]  Joel 2:32 [49]  James 4:8, Hebrews 10:22 [50]

# Acknowledgments and Short Bio

Thank you for reading *The Stone Writer.* I'd like to thank the people in my life who helped me publish this book. Most writers need a good editor to go over their stories and make helpful suggestions, spotting weaknesses in the story structure. I found a very good editor in Teresa Crumpton. She helped me polish my stories and make them shine. Thank you Teresa! I must also thank my grandchildren, who are the real inspiration for creating these short stories, and my four daughters who would love and support me, even if I all I ever wrote was bad poetry and driveling nonsense!

Thanks to my husband Kerry who initiated the art and graphics for the e-book version, as well as artist Bob Buckner for his vision and expertise in redesigning the graphic overlay for the paperback application. I also thank my sister Jacqui, and my husband Kerry who helped proof the manuscript. Last of all, a special thank you goes to my Mom, who always wanted to publish stories for kids but never got the chance. Here's to you, Mom.

Now a little background about me. I have been a hobby writer for many years. My first published articles featured stories about canoeing adventures on Minnesota lakes and rivers. Later in life, I decided to sign up for writing courses with the Institute of Children's Literature. For the first time, I learned how to write children's stories with the help of a talented instructor. Writing for children was a new adventure! As ideas began to come to mind, I finally had the tools I needed to develop them into real stories. I hope you have enjoyed reading my stories as much as I had writing them!

www.ingramcontent.com/pod-product-compliance
Lightning Source LLC
Chambersburg PA
CBHW031317040426
42443CB00005B/104